HAND
BOOKBINDING

A MANUAL OF INSTRUCTION

wax paper

buckram
cotton
linen
binder's board
book paper
bond paper

gummed tape

cloths

paste

linen tape

beeswax

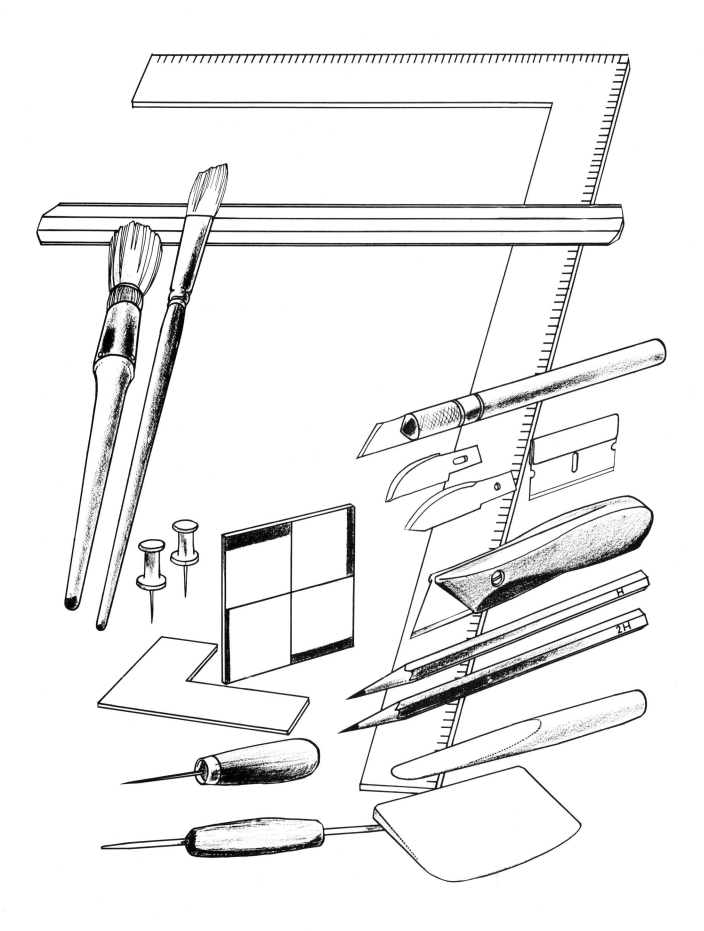

HAND
BOOKBINDING

A MANUAL OF INSTRUCTION

BY ALDREN A. WATSON

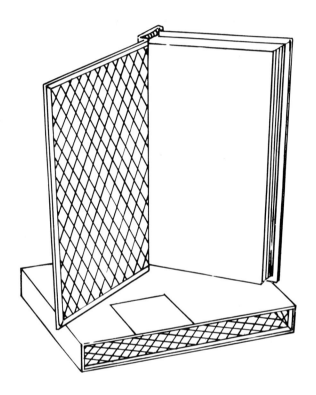

WITH *Illustrations by the* AUTHOR

BELL PUBLISHING COMPANY, INC.

NEW YORK

TO

EVA AULD WATSON *and* NANCY DINGMAN WATSON

*Both enthusiastic craftsmen, the one whose artistic
curiosity inspired my first binding; the other for
her uncompromising insistence upon integrity in
any art form.*

Designed by Aldren A. Watson

Printed in the United States of America
*This edition published by Bell Publishing Company, Inc.,
a division of Crown Publishers, Inc., by arrangement
with Reinhold Publishing Corporation.*
i j k l m n o p q

CONTENTS

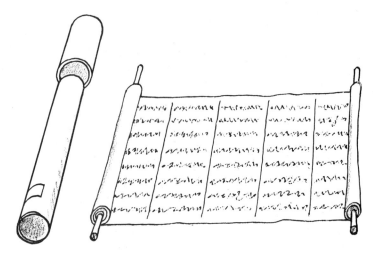

I

Introduction

PARADOXICALLY, THE HISTORY OF BOOKBINDing begins many centuries after the appearance of the first book. One of the earliest known "books" is a papyrus roll, dating from the twenty-fifth century, B.C. and containing 18 columns of Egyptian hieratic writing [FIG. 1]. The roll form continued throughout two thousand years of pre-Christian history. Even after the birth of Christ, although parchment replaced papyrus, the roll volume (from *volvere-* to roll) remained the standard form. But the arrangement of the writing in parallel columns separated by vertical lines held the potentiality for the development of a new form. Eventually, the idea of cutting the roll into separate panels, each holding three or four columns, gave birth to the book as we know it. The first bound book, then, was made up of single sheets, hinged along one edge by means of sewing or lacing. In the Latin codex, or manuscript book, the columnar arrangement of writing was continued; typical examples from Roman times have three or four columns to the page. Down to the present day, two- and three-column pages have proven practical and easy to read. Since modern trade books are predominantly single column, their pages are smaller, in contrast to the much larger books of earlier times.

Early bindings exhibited all of the basic construction elements which characterize bindings today. They were made up of folded sheets, collected into "gatherings," and sewn onto cords running across their backs. The leaves of the books were large, probably determined by the size of the animal skins from which the parchment was made [FIG. 2]. Subsequently, wooden boards were placed on either side of the book proper, in positions corresponding to the front and back covers. Then it was discovered that the cords onto which the signatures (sheets folded into pages) were sewn could as easily be laced directly into the edges of these boards to form a more compact and durable unit [FIG. 3]. The evolution of bookbinding was completed when the whole volume was covered with a sheet of leather to conceal the sewing and provide further reinforcement of the hinges [FIG. 4].

The history of bookbinding is at once simple and infinitely complex. In the past 1800 years there has not been one single change in the basic construction of the book, as an examination of a

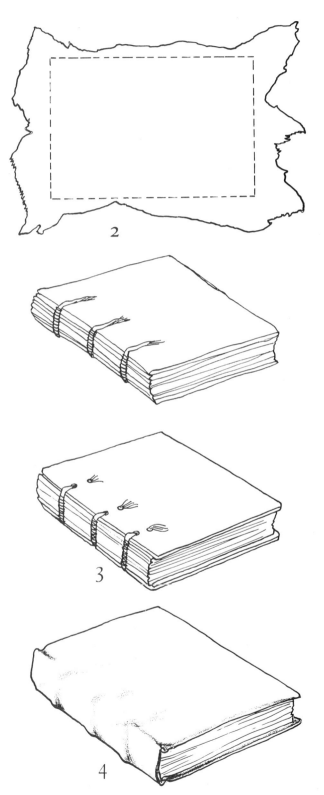

2

3

4

contemporary binding will reveal. It is still made up of a series of folded signatures, sewn together at the folds, and contained between two boards whose outer surfaces are covered. Just as the development of any technique cannot be isolated from concurrent factors, so bookbinding has been influenced by many events having nothing directly to do with books, or even literature.

The early monastic orders were the guardians of nearly all knowledge and culture in the Middle Ages, both with respect to writing and scholarship. Thus it is quite logical that the same persons to whom were intrusted the skills of reading and writing should also have fulfilled the function of bookbinders. The high standard of their craftsmanship attested to the thoroughness of their education; and this educated segment of the population was a decided minority. Hence, the beginnings of bookbinding are allied with the church, and concerned primarily with ecclesiastical literature and manuscript books whose principal functions were to serve the clergy. The large size of early manuscript writing determined the large page size and bulk of books of the period [FIG. 5]. They

Paper making was introduced to Europe from China in the tenth century. Sheets of this new handmade material approximated parchment in weight, although they could be folded, punched, and sewn with far greater flexibility. Good strong thread was used in the sewing, and silk was employed in making headbands. Leather was attached to the wooden cover boards in its full thickness; shaving it thin, or paring, as it is called, was unknown. If the temptation is to consider these bindings clumsy, they rather deserve the more proper term "rugged." For these binders worked in the tradition of their times; their durable bindings resulted simply from doing their work the only way they knew—well.

With the rapid spread of paper mills throughout Europe, it was discovered that large sheets of paper need not always be used as a single fold— or folio size. Paper could be folded again and again; two folds produced a page about 9 by 12 inches, or the quarto page; three folds made a very convenient size about 6 by 9 inches, or the octavo—eight leaves = sixteen pages [FIG. 7]. This latter size corresponds to the average book today.

6

5

Reed pen

were written and copied with infinite patience, skill, and labor. And as they were quite literally original works of art, early bindings were treasures in a very real sense. They were stored on shelves or chained to desks for safekeeping. They were ceremonial books, to be used by only a select few people. Large and attractively covered in fine leather, the boards of these early bindings invited man's instinct for decoration. Many examples exist of richly tooled covers, frequently decorated with settings of gems and rare stones or heavy gold leaf designs [FIG. 6]. As a further embellishment, engraved gold clasps were often fitted to the foreedges to hold the book shut when not in use. Working with the finest materials obtainable, and with unlimited time at their disposal, the monastery bookbinders turned out magnificent works whose chief virtues were uncompromising quality, heavy weight materials, and the best workmanship.

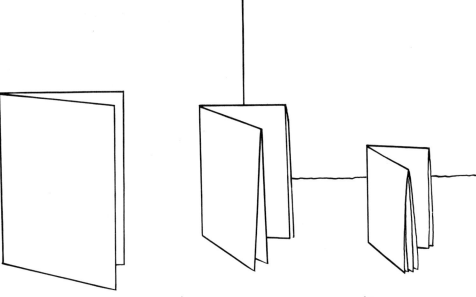

7

This pleasing discovery, when it was coupled with a new hunger among the growing educated classes for more books on a broad range of subjects, set the stage for a new phase in bookbinding.

The *revolution* in bookbinding started, however, in the middle of the fifteenth century with the invention of printing from movable type. A manuscript book, copied by hand, was the product of a slow process producing a single volume. With Gutenberg's process of composing words from individual type letters, an entire page could be set up and printed in a vastly accelerated manner. Relatively speaking, bookbinding changed from an individual craft to one of mass production. This did not immediately bring about a reduction in the size of books, for the early type faces were copied from the old, large calligraphic letters. The growing public demand for books provided the catalyst for a dramatic increase both in the quantity of books and the need for bookbinders.

Bookbinding was transferred from the monasteries to the printers' shops, and later to quite separate binding establishments. Leather persisted as the most suitable covering material, but the recently imported art of blind and gold tooling, long practiced in the East, gave bookbinding fresh impetus. The cords on which the signatures were sewn, and which were covered by the leather, made pleasing raised bands across the back of the volume. This feature was used as a design element by more or less filling the rectangular spaces between the bands with hand tooled designs, built up with impressions from several small hand tools [FIG. 8].

Europe's royal families and others of the aristocratic classes indirectly sponsored the development of distinct binding styles through their patronage and support of many skillful binders.

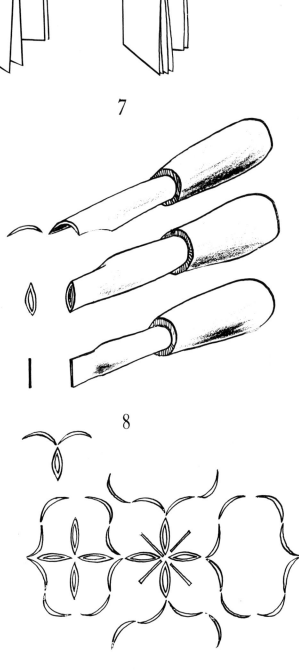

8

11

Coats of arms, crests, and family badges were customarily made a central feature of bindings done to order for their private libraries. Curiously, however, these binding styles are not known by the names of the binders, but by the names of the persons who commissioned the work. For example, there exists an enormous collection of "Grolier" bindings, named for Jean Grolier, Vicomte d'Aguisy, who was the treasurer of France in 1545.

The industrial revolution also left its mark on the bookbinding trade. In the early nineteenth century, paralleling the invasion by the machine of every conceivable manufacturing field, book-binding methods suffered radical and destructive innovations. Where formerly the tooling of designs in leather had been strictly a handcraft, whole panels of tooling were now stamped by machine in a single swift operation. While this put "fine binding" into the hands of every reader, the new machine stampings lacked taste and were not executed with the care characteristic of hand bind-ing. Rather than evolving a *new* type of binding decoration geared to speed and low cost, the machine attempted to give the appearance of hand binding without achieving handmade quality. This deliberate lowering of standards for the sake of price was also reflected in the use of cheaper paper, the recently introduced machine woven cloths, and short-cut binding methods. When flat tapes were introduced to replace cords, commer-cial bindings continued to be influenced by the traditional look of elegance, even to the extent of attaching false bands to the backbone [FIG. 9]. In true flexible leather binding, the leather is glued directly to the backs of the signatures. But a hollow back was invented for use with tape sewing, which at once thrust almost all the strain upon the two hinges, instead of evenly distributing it over the backs of the signatures.

The hollow back presaged the arrival of yet another "improvement," which eventually was to become responsible for further deterioration of binding methods. This was the invention of the *case binding*. To answer the demands for speed, the covers and backbones were made up quite independently of the sewn signatures, in one flat unit consisting of the two cover boards, the back-bone stiffener, and the cloth or paper cover material. All titling, decoration, and finishing was done while the case was flat. Then the sewn signatures and the case were brought together and fastened one to the other on a special machine. This modern advance harked back to the early Christian bindings, before a method had been devised for lacing the cords directly to the boards [FIG. 10].

By the late 1800's the book had become a

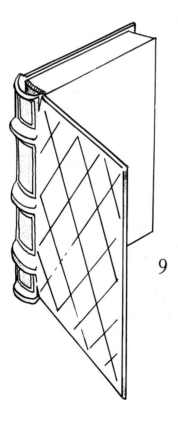

9

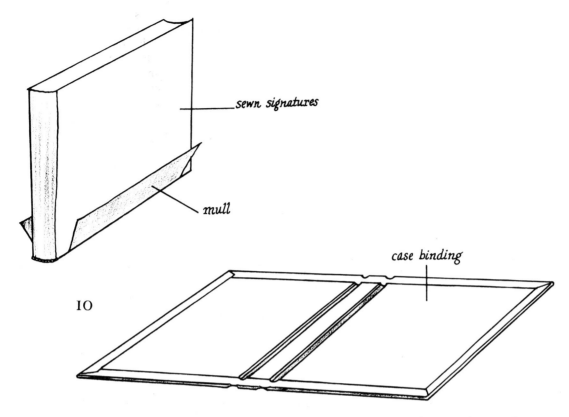

sewn signatures

mull

10

case binding

permanent democratic property. Machine methods had become firmly entrenched and had succeeded in producing unlimited numbers of books at popular prices. A reaction against the deterioration of quality occurred about mid-century in the formation of a group of capable printers and designers under the leadership of William Morris in England. An impressive list of craftsmen headed by T. J. Cobden-Sanderson established private presses or small printing shops. Handmade paper, hand-cut type punches, hand composition, presswork, and hand binding were the weapons these private presses adopted to combat the machine's insistence upon inferiority. This influential minority continued with a vigorous determination to produce fine books through a conscious return to the fundamentally sound practices which characterized early book manufacture.

To summarize, up until the seventeenth century—or approximately mid point between the invention of movable type and the arrival of machine techniques in the book trades—bookbinding had been a hand craft characterized by careful workmanship and the finest materials. Following the startling changes introduced by machine technology, books lacked artistic taste and utilitarian construction. Whereas all bookbinding had formerly been of high quality, fine binding became a specialized craft, divorced from commercial binding, and catering to collectors, li-

braries, private collections, and a small group of people who still appreciated good workmanship, not only with respect to the book's contents, but also its binding.

This book is presented as a manual for students and professionals in the fields of publishing, typography, paper making, engraving, type setting, printing, and binding. The instruction has been confined to the traditional methods basic to all types of binding and has not, for example, been extended to deal with leather binding, which is an advanced and specialized adjunct to the fundamentals described here. The text has been arranged to consider the logical sequence of binding procedures, commencing with the folding of paper and progressing through successive steps to a finished, complete binding. All the technical procedures are illustrated with diagrams where necessary to clarify any phase of bookbinding.

The purpose of this book is threefold: to describe clearly the basically simple procedures of fine bookbinding; to stimulate the revival already begun and gaining momentum of better binding practices, and to provide examples of how this exciting and useful art may be realistically related to the contemporary book fields.

A. A. W.
Putney, Vermont
1962

13

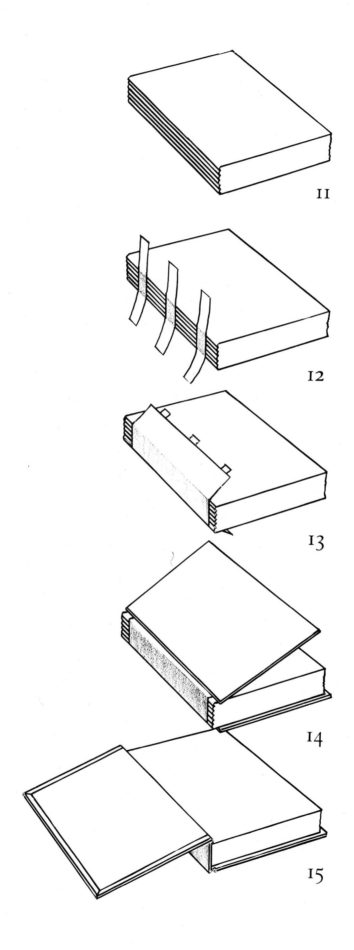

11

12

13

14

15

PART 1
General Procedure

HAND BINDING INVOLVES A FUNDAMENTALLY simple process which may be divided into five principal stages. Motivated by an interest in this eminently practical art, anyone with reasonable manual skill can successfully carry out the following steps in the construction of a good binding.

1. *Preparing the signatures* [FIG. 11] Assuming a blank notebook is to be bound, sheets of paper are cut and squared to a uniform size. The sheets are then folded into sections of three or four sheets each to make signatures. As each section is folded, a number is put on the back edge next to the fold to maintain the proper sequence. In other words, each section is "signed" —hence the term signature. As we have seen in reviewing the history of binding, the folding of the material on which the writing was placed created the change from a roll to a *binding*. The fold provides the foundation for sewing, which is the very heart of bookbinding.

2. *Sewing up the signatures* [FIG. 12] To bind all of the signatures into one flexible unit, each in its proper order is sewn firmly to a series of tapes (or cords, in the case of leather binding), running at right angles across the backs of the signatures. This operation places the folded backs of the signatures in a secure position, permitting each leaf of the book to turn freely.

3. *Gluing up the back* [FIG. 13] A reinforcement is now added to the backs of the sewn signatures in the form of a strip of cloth called *mull*. This is attached by means of binding paste (which has almost entirely replaced glue) applied to the backs of the signatures and worked down into the spaces between them. When the mull dries, the book proper is solidly unified and ready for the next step.

4. *Attaching the boards* [FIG. 14] A stiff cover board on either side of the sewn signatures is necessary for two reasons: to hold the leaves of the book flat and to protect the three exposed edges of the pages from damage and dirt. Boards are cut to a size slightly larger than the pages of the book and firmly attached with paste to the tapes and mull. The book will now rest on the edges of the boards, thus holding the pages clear and free from damage.

5. *Finishing* [FIG. 15] Since the exposed backs of the signatures and the sewing are subject to damage and soiling, a covering of cloth or paper (or leather) is pasted over the outside of the front cover board, around the backbone, and onto the outside of the back cover board. The edges of the covering material are turned under and pasted to the inside surfaces of both boards. As the final step in finishing, the first leaf of the first signature is pasted down to the inside of the front cover, and the last leaf of the last signature is pasted down in the same way. With these two *end sheets* attached, the book may be said to be bound.

These are the basic structural steps of every bookbinding. Further refinements, such as variations in materials used, dust jackets, slipcases, labeling, and the detailed elaboration of these five steps, are processes apart from the over-all binding process. They will be described fully in successive chapters.

Materials

The raw materials for bookbinding include paper, cloth, tape, thread, boards, and mull. Since the greatest investment in good binding is time itself, only the best materials should be used. The additional cost per book will be negligible because very little material goes into a single binding.

Rag papers, or rag content papers, are best for making signatures in a blank book. White bond paper is excellent for this, as well as a wide variety of imported paper handmade especially for such purposes as bookbinding. These papers are available in white, cream, and various intermediate shades, which make it possible to match new papers to those already used in a book being rebound. There are also many beautiful imported papers printed with handsome patterns; these are well suited to the purposes of covering or lining the boards.

There are three types of cloth for use in bookbinding: cotton fabrics, which can be bought in an almost unlimited range of colors, patterns, and weights; linens; and buckram, which is a specially woven binder's cloth filled with a sizing. It should be pointed out that buckram, being quite

15

stiff, is more difficult to work with and is not available to the hand bookbinder in the interesting colors found in cotton or linen.

Regular binder's board is best for making cover boards and the backbone board. It is tough and more resistant to warping than common cardboard or pasteboard. For very small books, the best grades of artists' illustration board, which is made in a thinner weight, work very well. They come in single and double ply. This board is especially good for making slipcases.

Linen tape, which is available in various widths, is far superior to cotton for sewing up the signatures. Two widths are sufficient for most work —one about ¼ inch wide and another ⅜ inch wide. The width of tape should, of course, be determined by the size of the book to be bound. Three wide tapes would be needed for a thick book of fair size while two narrow ones would be best for a slender volume of poetry.

Bookbinding thread should be used instead of ordinary sewing threads, which are hard and sharp. Binder's thread is strong, but soft and pliable. Thread should always be waxed before use.

Mull, the cloth strip pasted up the backs of the sewn signatures, can best withstand wear and tear if it is cut from a piece of good quality linen. The ordinary mull marketed for bookbinders is too flimsy and soon breaks down after the binding has been used a little. A yard or two of linen will bind a good many books.

The entire list of materials may be obtained from a binding supply house or pieced together from the stocks of art materials dealers, hardware stores, or department stores. A complete listing of suppliers of materials and tools can be found on page 93. Before using any material in actual binding, it is a wise precaution first to test a sample—a piece of cloth for example—to determine how it behaves with the paste you are using. The sample should be pasted and allowed to dry before deciding on its suitability.

Tools and Equipment

The list of tools and equipment includes many items which may already be at hand or easily obtained. A steel carpenter's square is essential for accurate cutting of all materials. Two pencils for marking (an H and a 2H), a common steel-edge ruler for measuring, and one or two good knives will facilitate all of the preliminary steps. In experienced hands, a single-edge razor blade performs very well. The mat-cutting knife with interchangeable blades is possibly the best cutting tool. A small carborundum stone on which to sharpen all cutting edges is recommended. A good pair of shears is necessary for cutting cloth.

A flat wooden folder of the type illustrated is best for folding signature paper or other large sheets. The round-end folding stick and the folding needle perform special folding jobs more easily and in a neater manner.

A squared card, either of cardboard or, still better, metal, is a required aid for squaring up the backs of signatures prior to sewing.

A sewing frame is essential for workmanlike binding. It is composed of a flat platform with perpendicular posts supporting a cross rod to which the tapes are fastened during sewing. Likewise, a finishing press facilitates many of the important operations of binding, such as gluing up and attaching the boards.

Special formula bookbinding paste, by far the best adhesive, is available in jars or cans of different sizes. Vegetable glue is also quite satisfactory; both of these pastes are permanent and remain somewhat flexible. Animal derivative glues tend to become brittle when dry, causing cracking. Two paste brushes will be needed: one round binding brush for general pasting and a No. 5 oil painting bristle brush for finer work, such as turning over the edges of cloth. Only top quality brushes work well; soft, limp bristles do not spread the paste evenly.

Miscellaneous equipment includes an awl or two, a cake of beeswax, fine sandpaper, a package of No. 4 needles, wide mouth water jars, wastepaper, and a supply of cut magazine sheets for rubbing pasted work dry.

Bookbinding supply houses stock a complete list of all these tools and equipment. Art supply stores and hardware and department stores can supply many of the items, and many of the tools can be made in the workshop from readily available woods and metals. Before buying everything ready made, you may wish to consider which tools you can manufacture yourself. The two most critical pieces of equipment are the sewing frame and the finishing press, both of which can be bought from a binding supplier. These tools are made of fine materials and will last indefinitely. In many instances, group buying can effect some discounts on prices. Part 5 contains instruction for the home manufacture of many of the tools described.

Workspace

Throughout the book, the surface on which binding is done will be referred to as the work bench, or *bench*. An ideal bench would be about 30 inches wide and eight feet long. One long table can be arranged for the three work spaces; but two or three separate tables will do as well (see back end sheets). Cover all work surfaces with brown wrapping paper stretched flat and taped to the bench on all four sides. The right-hand section is organized for cutting and folding, the center section for sewing and finishing, and the left-hand section for all pasting operations. The finishing press may be lifted off the bench when not in use. Lay a large sheet of heavy cardboard or hardboard over the cutting section to protect the bench from knife cuts. Have a large carton or two nearby for wastepaper.

Clean, neat work habits are important for successful binding. A supply of clean cloths should be prepared in advance and stacked at the back of the bench. Keep a jar or two of clean water on the bench, also a separate cloth for removing paste spots, washing the hands, and keeping tools clean. Trim the folded edges from a stack of clean newspapers and pile the sheets ready for use on the paste section. Trim off the stapled backbone of a large magazine to provide a supply of rubbing sheets. Now arrange your tools along the back of the bench next to the appropriate sections.

If possible set up a separate smaller bench equipped for pressing bindings during the various work stages. A few heavy books (such as encyclopedias) or a small marble slab will make excellent weights. Have an extra carton under the bench for soiled wastepaper. Pasting operations are done briskly, and a long trip to the wastebasket may prove costly! Keep all work surfaces spotlessly clean: good binding cannot be done in an untidy place.

Good lighting is important for accurate work during all phases of bookbinding. A long fluorescent tube or a pair of drop lights will furnish sufficient illumination. If the work benches cannot be left intact when not in use, store the tools and other pieces of equipment in clearly marked cartons to keep them clean.

Technical Methods

Measuring. The first step in good binding is accurate measuring. The ruler and one side of the carpenter's square are graduated in sixteenths of an inch. Whether measuring paper, boards, cloth, or buckram, make it a rule to be precise. If the dimensions you are working with do not fall exactly on these divisions of the ruler and square, use a strip of white paper. Mark the dimensions on this strip with a 2H pencil, then transfer the marks to the material to be cut [FIG. 16].

Cutting. Follow accurate measuring with equally careful cutting. Handmade binding papers and many machine-made papers are not always square on the corners. The material must be squared up before cutting to size, regardless of whether it is paper, board, or cloth. Lay the short side of the square even with one edge of the

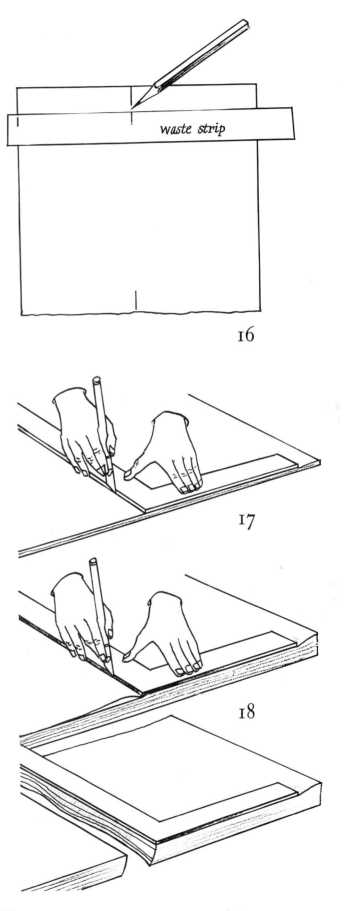

waste strip

16

17

18

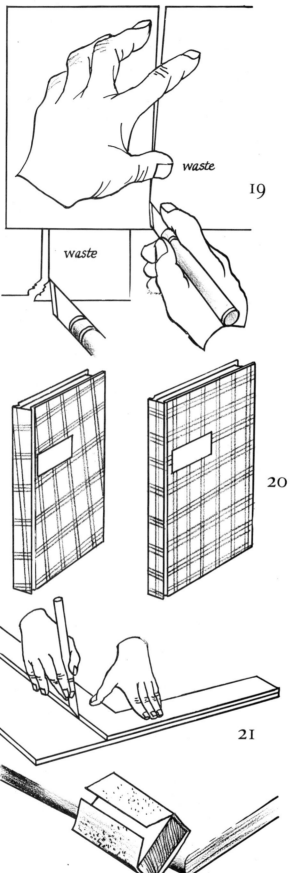

waste

waste

19

20

21

material to be cut. Holding the square down tightly with the left hand, cut along the other side of the square with the knife [FIG. 17]. If you are working with paper, cut only a few sheets at a time. For example, if 20 sheets are to be cut, cut them in lots of five sheets each. Cutting the whole lot at once will result in wavy, uneven edges which will render the paper worthless, since good folding cannot be done with crooked paper [FIG. 18]. Use a *light* pressure on the knife. Make many light cuts rather than a few heavy ones. Keep firm pressure on the square at all times. When cutting only one or two sheets, hold down the top edge of the waste with a finger to prevent tearing out the corner at the end of the stroke [FIG. 19].

Decorated or patterned papers which are used for end papers, lining the boards, or as cover paper should be cut so that the direction of the pattern lines up with the edge of the finished work. A paper mask may be useful in determining the cutting position [FIG. 20].

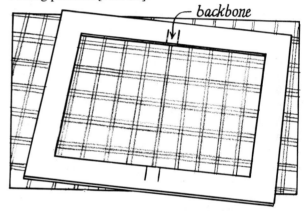

— backbone

Binder's board is harder and more dense than ordinary cardboard. When cutting boards, use the square held tightly in alignment with one edge of the board. Keep the knife perpendicular, and make many light cuts [FIG. 21]. A square, clean edge can be obtained easily in this way. Wavy-edged boards cannot be nicely finished; the cover material will go on badly and spoil the whole appearance. After cutting, sandpaper the edges of the board to remove the sharp edge. This creates a better appearance as well as a longer lasting job. A round edge is far less liable to damage than a sharp one.

Cloth may be cut with the knife and square or with shears. If the square is used, it must be held down very tightly to prevent the cloth from "creeping" [FIG. 22]. The grain of some cloth is uniform enough so that cutting along a thread with the shears will give accurate results. Fabrics with a printed design or pattern should be cut with the direction of the pattern parallel to the edge of the finished work, as in the case of patterned paper [FIG. 23].

Buckram can be cut in the same manner as paper. However, the selvage edge should be trimmed off first. The selvage is the finished edge, often having the appearance of a narrow tape. Because it is of a texture different from the rest of the buckram, and somewhat bulky, it is discarded.

Pasting. Bookbinding involves many pasting operations, from attaching the mull to pasting down the end sheets in the final stage of binding. Without exception, *always* lay the work to be pasted on top of the newspaper waste sheets. As soon as the work has been brushed with paste, pick it up and throw the soiled wastepaper into the carton. This is one of the most vital habits to establish at the very outset.

The aim in pasting is to spread a *thin,* even coat of paste over the surface of the work. Blobs and streaks of paste will prevent the material from lying flat, or they will trap bubbles of air under the work when it is stuck down. In either instance the finished work will not be smooth.

Spreading paste on paper, board, cloth, or buckram should be accomplished by starting in the center of the work [FIG. 24]. There are two reasons for this: it allows the free hand to hold down the work without becoming sticky, and it delivers paste to the edges of the work last. Thus, the edges may be expected to stick securely. Pasting should be done briskly, though not hurriedly. If the paste is spread too slowly, portions of the pasted work may be partly dry before the work is stuck down, and a good tight job will not result.

The way in which a piece of pasted paper is stuck down is also of great importance. Three things should be borne in mind: paper which has been pasted is wet and will therefore expand. Prompt handling is necessary so that it may be stuck down before too much expansion takes place. Air bubbles are often trapped under the paper as it is laid down, and these must be eliminated. Last but not least, any excess paste that gets on the finished work will cause trouble. To keep these factors under control, the following procedure is recommended: As soon as the paste has been spread, pick up the work and lay it paste-side-down on the surface to which it is being attached. Immediately, lay over the work a clean rubbing (magazine) sheet. With a clean cloth, start rubbing the pasted paper down firmly, working from the center outward to all four sides [FIG. 25]. This motion pushes any air bubbles out from under the paper. The rubbing sheet prevents soiling the surface of the work, and provides a shiny surface for the cloth to glide over. When the work is firmly rubbed down, discard the rubbing sheet. It would be worthwhile to perform a few trial pasting jobs using scrap paper and board to estab-

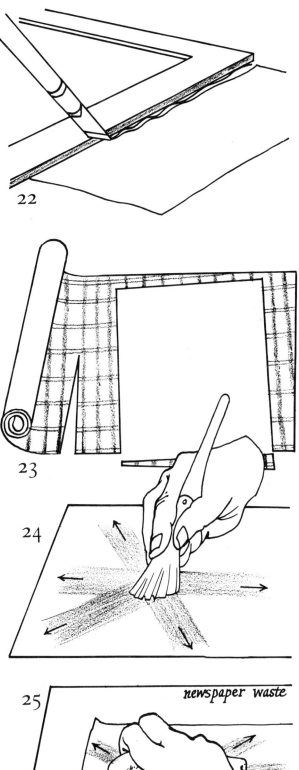

22

23

24

25

newspaper waste

rubbing sheet laid over work

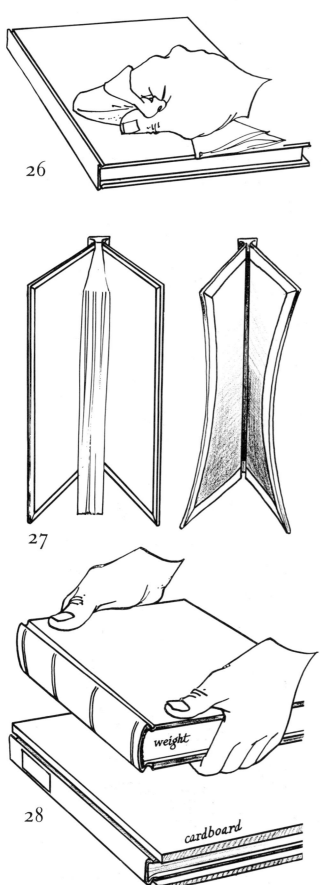

26

27

weight

cardboard

28

lish this sequence of movements before attempting any finished work. Finally, inspect the work. If there are any spots of paste on it, moisten a corner of a clean cloth with saliva and gently wipe off the paste [FIG. 26].

Pressing. Putting a piece of pasted work under weights is not a separate step, but the final stage of pasting. To understand the function of pressing, it should be made clear that a piece of paper or cloth which has been pasted begins to expand at once. It literally stretches out in size. Accordingly, as the paste dries, the paper or cloth shrinks back to its original size. It is clearly seen that if in the meantime the paper or cloth has been attached to a board, for example, then the board will be bent or warped as the paper shrinks. This is perfectly normal; however, in bookbinding the pasted work must be held under control *until the expansion and shrinkage has stopped.* Placing the freshly pasted work under heavy weights will hold everything in its proper position. It is true that some warping will still take place, as in the case binding in FIG. 27. But when the end sheets have been pasted down inside both cover boards, this counter pull will bring the boards back to their original flat positions.

Put the work in press in the following manner: place a clean sheet of waxed paper flat on the bench. Paste will not stick to the wax surface. Then lay the work just completed down on the waxed paper, and lay a second piece over the work. Now place heavy weights—several large books or the marble slab—on top. Allow the work to stay in press until it is dry. The length of time for complete drying will depend on the size and character of the operation pasted. A good rule of thumb is to leave the work in press overnight, unless it is an intermediate pasting job. For example, a case binding to which the cover material has been attached need remain under weights only for an hour before attaching the case to the book proper. As a general rule it is better to leave the work in press longer than seems necessary; taking the work out of press for an impatient inspection may cause undue warping, which is difficult to correct. Before going into the press, a finished binding should be protected with a piece of cardboard laid over each cover board, but not projecting over the joints [FIG. 28]. This prevents crushing the joints. In every case, protect any work by placing sheets of waxed paper on both sides of it.

PART 2

The Basic Steps

IN PART 1 WE OUTLINED THE GENERAL PRO-
cedure required for binding a book and discussed
the technical methods for the proper handling of
binding materials. Now, we are concerned with
the detailed performance of the actual binding
operations. The following steps are fundamental
to nearly all binding projects, even though individual bindings may require special modifications
of these basic steps.

1. FOLDING

The entire structure of bookbinding depends
on folding: the folded signature provides the
foundation for sewing, which in turn unites all
the leaves of the book into a flexible whole. Accurate folding is basic to the preparation of signatures and to other binding procedures which will
be discussed in Part 3. The leaves of the book
must turn freely, and the top edges should be as
smooth as possible to prevent the accumulation
of dust; these two requirements demand careful
folding.

Since the top edges of the pages must be as
even as possible, establish the habit of working
with the top edge of the paper toward you. Fold
from the right to the left (unless you are left-
handed). The left hand guides the edges of the
sheet into alignment and holds them there, while
the right hand makes the fold. Use the flat folder
for this type of folding. It does a job superior to
that done with the fingers and keeps the work
clean.

Single Fold

Using ordinary typewriter paper, make a few
trial single folds in this way: lay a sheet of paper
on the bench, with the top edge toward you [FIG.
29]. While holding down the left half of the sheet,
pick up the right side of the paper with the right
hand and roll it over to the left [FIG. 30]. Then,
guide the corners into even alignment with the
right hand. Hold them together tightly. With the
right thumb, press down to make a short crease
[FIG. 31]. Hold the top edges in alignment. With
the flat folder held in the right hand, run a crease
away from you the full length of the sheet. This
is a single fold [FIG. 32].

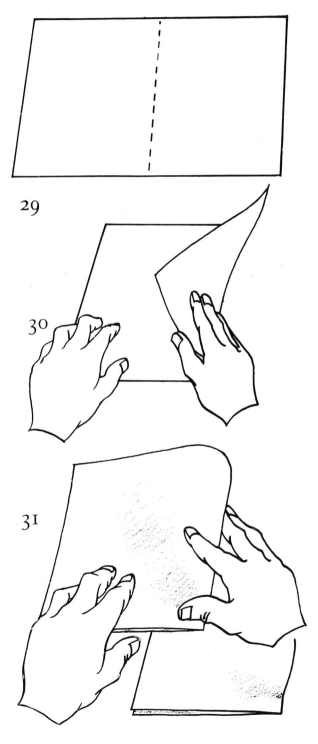

29

30

31

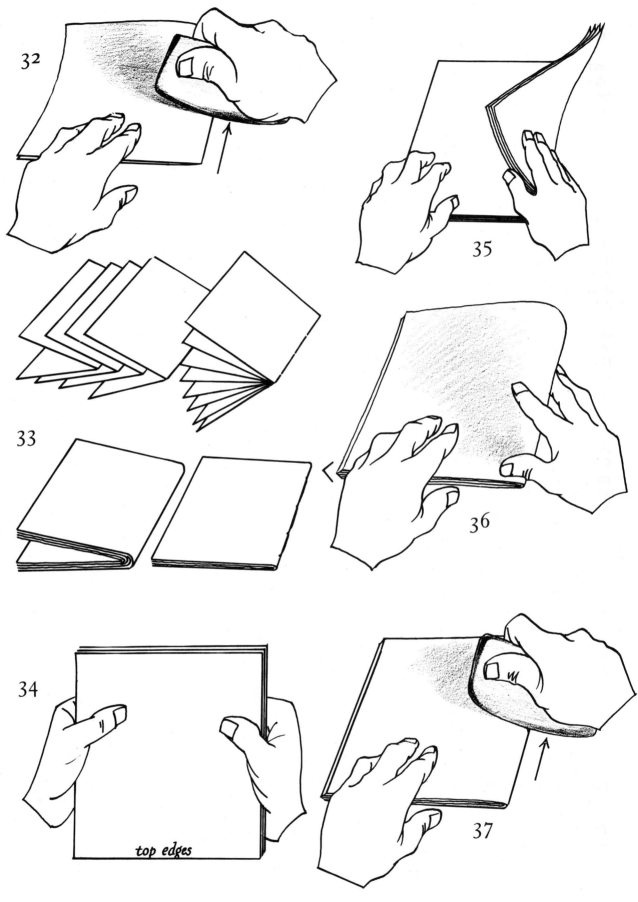

32

33

34

top edges

35

36

37

Folding a Signature

A signature consists of more than one folded sheet—usually four to six sheets. This bulk provides the backing necessary for strong sewing. All the sheets for one signature must be folded as a single unit. If the sheets are folded individually and then put together, they will cause the book to spring open after the sewing has been done [FIG. 33]. To make a trial signature, cut four sheets of white bond paper 8 by 10 inches, to be folded into a 5 by 8 inch signature. Gather up the cut sheets and tap their top edges gently on the bench for alignment [FIG. 34].

Now, lay the gathered sheets on the bench, top edges facing you. Holding the left half of the sheets firmly with the left hand, pick up all four sheets and roll them over to the left [FIG. 35]. The motion of folding is the same as for a single fold: it will take a little practice to guide four sheets into proper alignment so that all eight leaves line up. Now start the crease with the right thumb [FIG. 36]. The left-hand edges will form a slight "V." Hold down the work with the left hand, and finish the crease with the folder, as before [FIG. 37].

French Fold

The French fold is often used to add bulk to the binding of a single printed item, such as a short poem or similar brief work. Make a trial French fold as follows: single-fold a sheet of white bond paper, as described above. Then turn the folded side toward you. Pick up the doubled sheet by the right corner, and roll it over to meet the left corner. Align the top edges (which are now folds). A box may form at the corner due to the double thickness of paper [FIG. 38]. In this case, insert the end of the folding stick, pull the box out with pressure toward the right, then make the usual starting crease with the thumb [FIG. 39]. Hold the edges firmly in alignment and finish the crease with the flat folder.

As a preliminary to folding signatures for a finished binding, make several of these trial folds, using cheap paper. Practice folding single folds, signatures, and French folds until you can manipulate the paper easily and perform the work without flaws. A batch of paper used in this way will be well invested.

2. COLLATING

This term means to examine and verify the proper order of all the contents of a binding, including the signatures and any special material such as inserts, new end sheets, maps, or additions. Even in the case of a blank book, each signature should be numbered as it is folded. Starting with the first signature, mark a number next to the fold at the foot (bottom) of the outside leaf [FIG. 40].

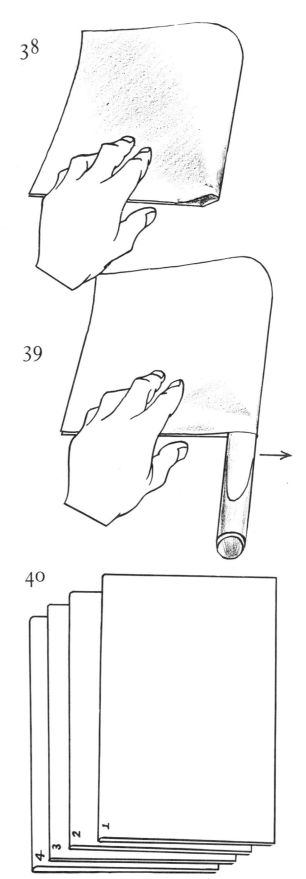

38

39

40

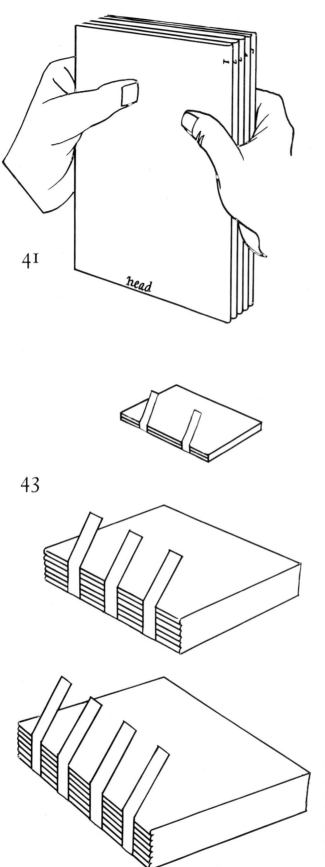

41

43

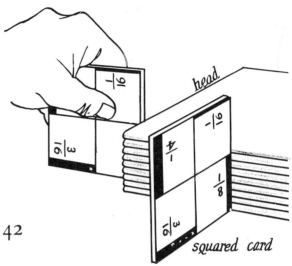

42

squared card

If an old book is being rebound, first go through the entire contents to make sure the sequence and position of all the material is correct. Make sure nothing is upside down! During this collating procedure, check the folios, or page numbers, at the same time. If new end sheets have been added to an old book, collate these as well. Finally, number each signature consecutively, starting with the first in the book. These numbers are a simple, accurate means of checking the work as it is sewn together.

3. MARKING UP AND SEWING ON TAPES

Marking up is the first stage of sewing. Pencil lines are drawn across the backs of all the signatures to indicate the position of the tapes and to provide guide marks for punching holes for the needle and thread to pass through. All the holes are punched before sewing is begun.

To mark up, first gather up all the signatures and tap the top edges down lightly on the bench [FIG. 41]. This is to even up the head, or top, of the book. Even up the head and back, using the squared card [FIG. 42]. Lay a weight on the signatures to prevent slipping. (A brick, wrapped and taped inside clean paper, makes a serviceable weight). As the pencil marks indicate the position of the tapes, it should first be determined how many tapes are needed. Generally speaking, a small volume—for example, a slim book of poetry with no more than four signatures—requires only two ⅜-inch tapes. An average novel or book of similar size should be sewn onto a pair of ½-inch tapes. Large books with many signatures, or a large page size, or both, should have three or possibly even four tapes. The factors of weight and proportion are to be considered, although it is better to use a heavier tape than may appear necessary [FIG. 43].

24

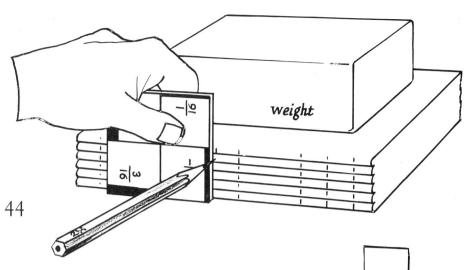

44

For the purposes of demonstration, let us assume the work is to be marked up for three tapes. There should be six marks drawn across the backs of the signatures, i.e., a mark either side of each tape. There must also be another mark at the head and a similar one at the foot where the thread passes from one signature over to the next. This stitch, which "catches up" the following signature, has come to be called a *kettle stitch*. Start with the head kettle stitch. Hold the squared card flat against the backs of the signatures, and draw a line across all of them, ½ inch from the head. Draw a similar line at the foot, ½ inch from the bottom. Now space the three tapes between these kettle stitch marks, and draw a pair of lines for each tape [FIG. 44].

The two marks for each tape should be spaced slightly wider than the width of the tape, so that during sewing the tape will not pucker [FIG. 45].

The next step is to punch all the holes in the signatures. This is done to make guide holes for the needle and thread, and it should be done before sewing in order for the holes to be centered on the folds of the signatures. Open the first signature flat, holding the folded sheets firmly [FIG. 46]. With a small awl, punch a hole at each pencil mark, punching from the outside to the center of the signature. Let the point of the awl go through all the sheets, but do not push the awl through clear to the handle. The hole should be a little smaller than the needle so that the paper will grip the thread. This will insure a tight sewing job. Punch all the signatures in the same way. When you have done this, lay the signatures face up on the bench.

The final preparation for sewing is setting up the sewing frame. This is a simple device which

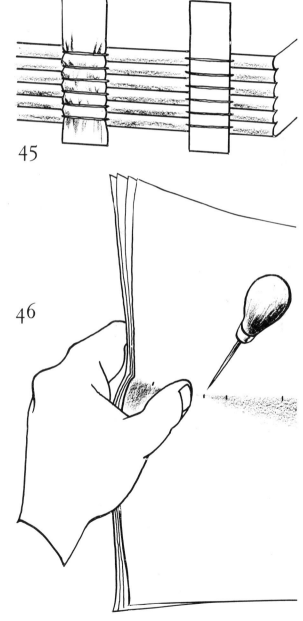

45

46

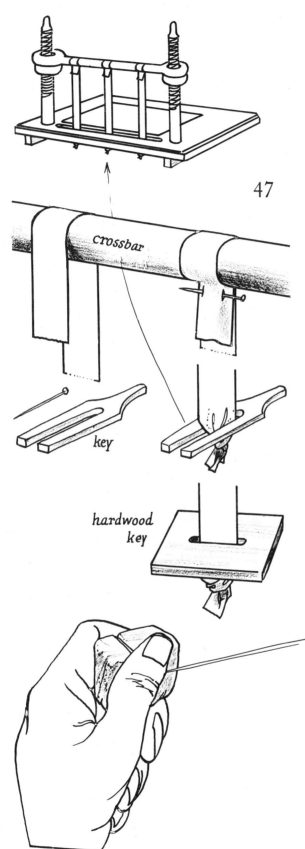

47

crossbar

key

hardwood
key

holds the tapes in a vertical position during sewing, leaving both hands free for work. Refer to the diagram [FIG. 47] for detailed method of putting on the tapes. Cut the tape into lengths of about 10 inches. This will allow ample space between the platform and the cross bar, with enough extra to tie the ends to the keys and cross bar. Even if you are sewing a very slim book, do not lower the cross bar too much: it is important to have a good view of the work. Any excess of tape beyond the actual sewing will be trimmed off later. Tighten up the cross bar enough to bring the tapes up taut, but not puckered. To line up the tapes, lay one signature on the platform, and adjust all the tapes to conform to the pencil marks on the signature. Check this alignment at the top next to the cross bar as well. Also, be sure the tapes are at right angles to the platform.

The sewing may now be done. Thread a needle with a 30-inch length of thread which has first been waxed. Waxing permits drawing the thread through more easily, prevents kinking, and extends its life. Draw the thread over the cake of beeswax two or three times, holding it tight against the wax with the thumb. Thread and needle size are determined by the thickness of the signatures and the firmness of the paper, as well as by the size and character of the book. Select a good binding thread of a suitable gauge. Common sewing thread is generally hard and may gash the paper where it passes through a hole. Tie a knot in the end of the waxed thread, leaving a two-inch tail beyond the knot.

Sewing is done from back to front: place the *last* signature on the sewing frame, with the folded edge touching the tapes. Make sure that the pencil marks line up with the tapes. Hold the right hand inside the center of the signature so the entering needle will not tear the paper. Take the needle in at the foot kettle stitch hole [FIG. 48]. Draw the thread up snug against the knot. Take the needle out again through the hole below the bottom tape. Now take the needle *over* the tape, and in again at the next hole above the tape. This is the basic principle of sewing, the means of fastening the tapes to the backs of the signatures. Proceed sewing in and out, passing the thread *over each tape* in turn, and finally coming out at the head kettle stitch hole as illustrated [FIG. 49]. Draw the thread up snug, but not too tight; *the sewing must be flexible!* Lay the next-to-the-last signature on top of the one just sewn. Open it to the center and slide your right hand inside. Take the needle in at the head kettle stitch hole, then sew in and out as before, bringing the needle out at the foot kettle stitch hole, just in line with the knot [FIG. 50]. You are now ready to tie the first kettle stitch. Pick up the knotted tail of thread with the left hand and

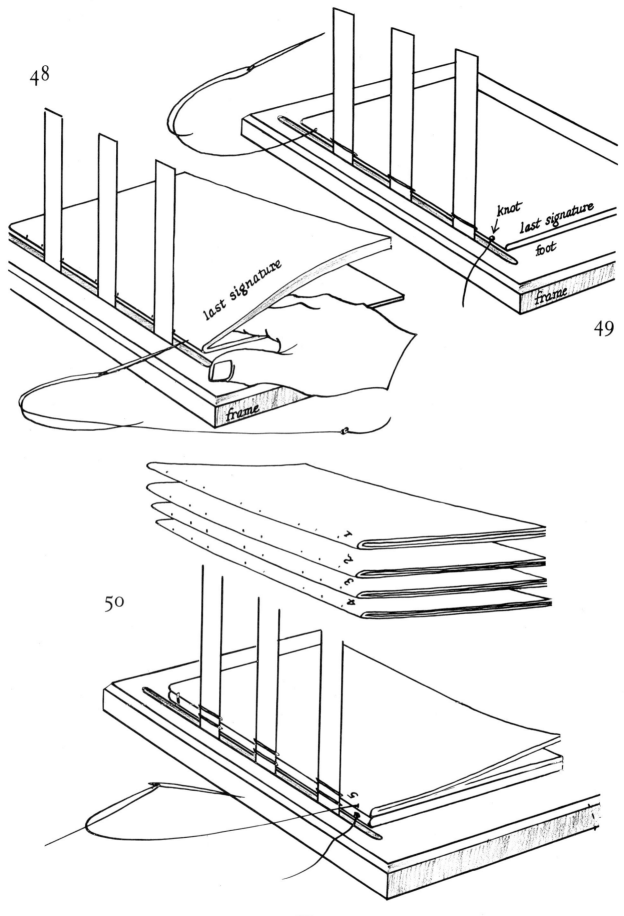

48

49

knot
last signature
last signature
foot

frame

last signature

frame

50

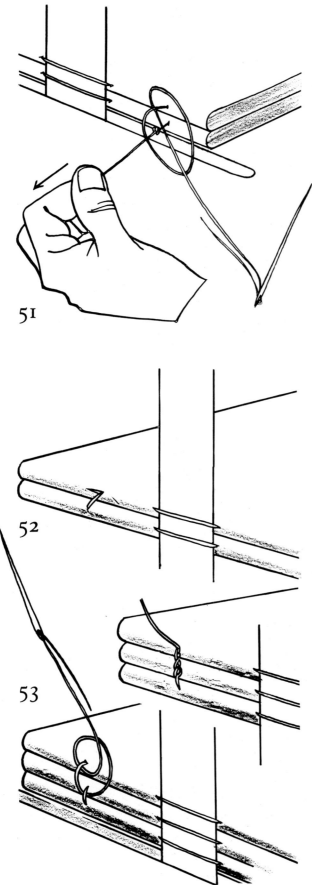

51

52

53

throw a loop around and *under the knot*. Then pass the needle through this loop and draw it up into a snug stitch [FIG. 51]. In drawing the thread tight at the completion of each signature, avoid too much tension, lest the signature paper tear back and weaken the construction [FIG. 52].

Now sew on the remaining signatures in the same way. Note that the next kettle stitch, and all the remaining ones, are done with the needle as illustrated [FIG. 53]. Reasonably snug stitches hold the signatures securely and at the same time allow maximum flexibility in the finished binding. If they are drawn too tight the back of the book will cave in [FIG. 54].

When the sewing is completed, tie off the last signature with a double knot. Trim the thread off, leaving a ¼-inch tail. Cut the tapes off the frame, and trim each of them to within two inches of the book. Pull the tapes out smooth from both sides in order to eliminate bunching between the threads [FIG. 55]. On a very thick book with a great many signatures a swelling may occur, due to the thickness of the threads lying in the centers of the signatures. Some of this may be reduced by tying together the threads along the backbone where they pass over the center tape [FIG. 56]. Groups of four or five threads may be tied in this way, but do not gather too many in each knot, as this may cause the paper to tear [FIG. 56]. (See also Knocking Down Swelling, p. 65.)

4. SQUARING THE HEAD AND GLUING UP

The function of these two steps is to stabilize the backbone into one flexible unit which is square. Even though the sewing unites all the signatures, *gluing up* holds them in proper relation so that when the book closes, the backbone returns to its proper shape. The term gluing up formerly referred to the specific use of glue, but in modern binding flexible pastes have been adopted in its place. Gluing up, then, means attaching with paste a strip of cloth lengthwise along the sewn signatures to reinforce the sewing.

At this stage, just after sewing the signatures, the book will have a tendency to gape open between the first and second signatures, and similarly between the last two signatures. To prevent this, these two pairs of signatures are lightly pasted together along the back edges. Lay the sewn signatures face up on the bench. Open to the division between the first and second signatures, laying the first signature over on a board for support. Place a clean sheet of waste paper on top of the second signature, leaving a band of the hinge uncovered, ⅛ inch wide. Brush a light coat of paste along this band [FIG. 57]. Remove the waste sheet, close the first signature back into place, and press down along the hinge. Turn the sewn signa-

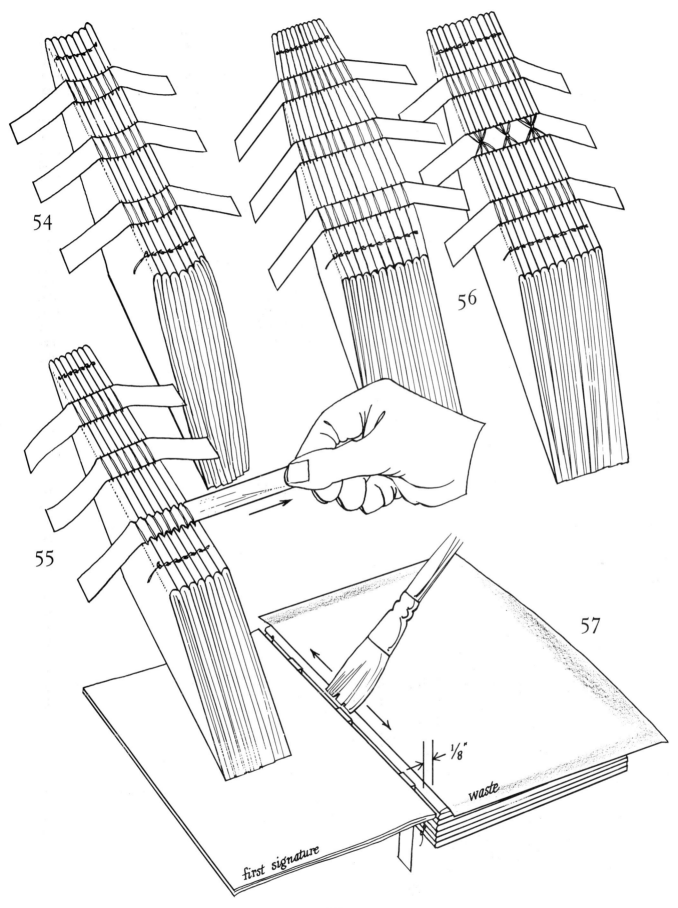

54

55

56

57

1/8"

waste

first signature

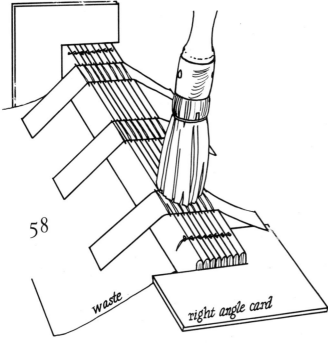

58

waste

right angle card

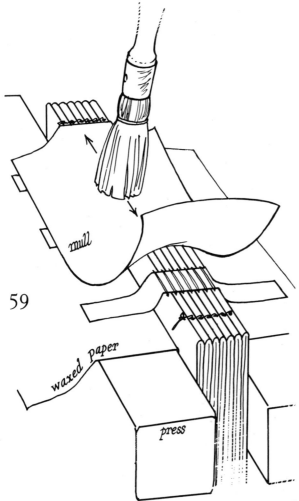

59

mull

waxed paper

press

tures over, and proceed to paste the last two signatures together in this same way.

The cloth strip which is next pasted to the backs of the signatures is called the mull. It covers all the sewing and projects on both sides of the book to form flaps, which with the tapes are the means of attaching the cover boards. Cut a piece of linen mull one inch shorter than the height of the book, and the width across the backbone, plus a two-inch overhang for each side. Next, square up the head in the following way: put a sheet of waxed paper on either side of the signatures, and then place them in the finishing press with the backbone projecting about ½ inch above the press. Tighten the press enough to hold the work. With the right-angle card (see p. 91) make the head square, and also square across the backs of the signatures [FIG. 58]. Now tighten the press. Lay the mull on a sheet of wastepaper, and brush paste over it, working the paste well into the weave. Then brush paste onto the backs of the signatures, working it into the tapes, and down between the signatures. Smooth out any lumps of paste. The object is to paste thoroughly, but not to build up a thick layer which will crack and weaken the binding later. Lay the mull paste side down on the backbone. Check all four sides to make sure it is centered [FIG. 59]. There should be a ½-inch space at both the head and foot. Rub the mull down tightly in place, especially over the tapes. Give the mull another very light brushing of paste. It may be necessary to work the mull down with the fingertips, to obtain a tight attachment over the tapes and between the signatures. Do not paste the loose ends of the tapes, but leave them hanging free. Wash hands following this operation. Leave the work in the finishing press overnight.

5. MAKING BOARDS

The cover boards form a buffer to protect the pages from damage and dust, and to keep the sewing from being damaged; they also hold the pages flat. Further protection is provided by the overhanging edges of the boards. This overhang, or *square*, absorbs any damaging blows and prevents the pages from touching the bookshelf. The boards are in three parts: front cover, back cover, and a narrow board to run up the backbone.

Although from the standpoint of durability there is a minimum thickness of board which should be used, keep in mind that the heavier the book, the thicker the board. A book with a large page size, for example, requires a heavier board in order to withstand the warping action of the paste. In general, use the minimum weight board for a very thin book, and thicker boards in ratio to the increased weight and size of larger volumes.

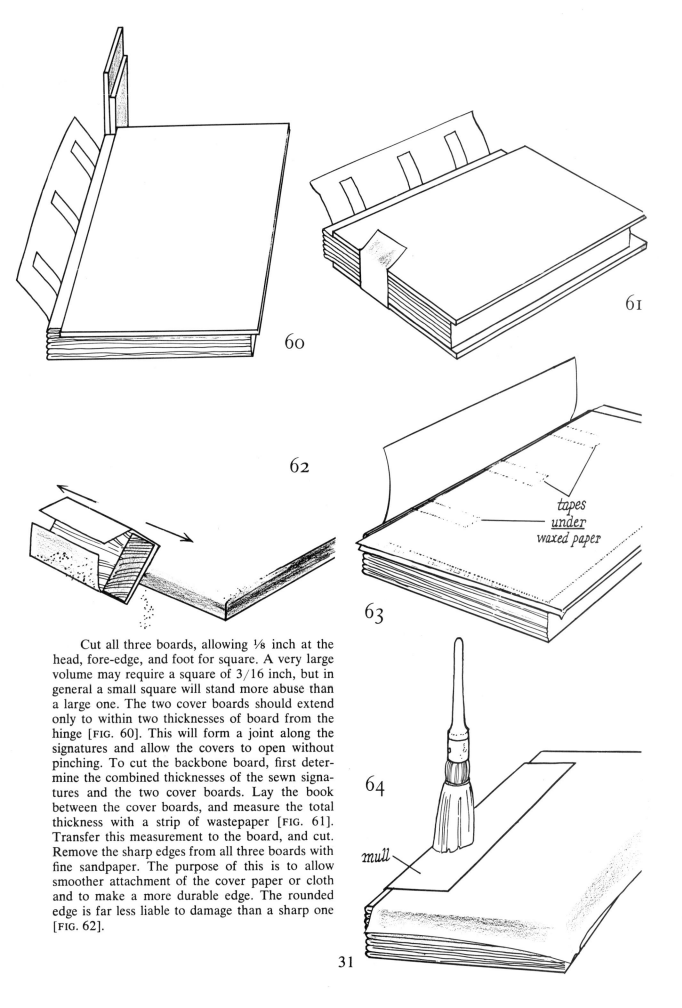

60

61

62

63

tapes
under
waxed paper

64

mull

Cut all three boards, allowing ⅛ inch at the head, fore-edge, and foot for square. A very large volume may require a square of 3/16 inch, but in general a small square will stand more abuse than a large one. The two cover boards should extend only to within two thicknesses of board from the hinge [FIG. 60]. This will form a joint along the signatures and allow the covers to open without pinching. To cut the backbone board, first determine the combined thicknesses of the sewn signatures and the two cover boards. Lay the book between the cover boards, and measure the total thickness with a strip of wastepaper [FIG. 61]. Transfer this measurement to the board, and cut. Remove the sharp edges from all three boards with fine sandpaper. The purpose of this is to allow smoother attachment of the cover paper or cloth and to make a more durable edge. The rounded edge is far less liable to damage than a sharp one [FIG. 62].

31

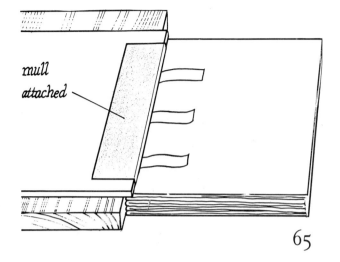

mull attached

65

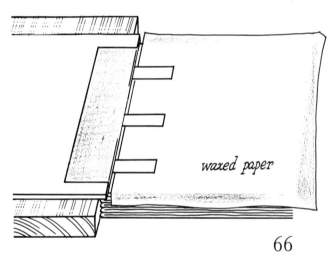

waxed paper

66

67

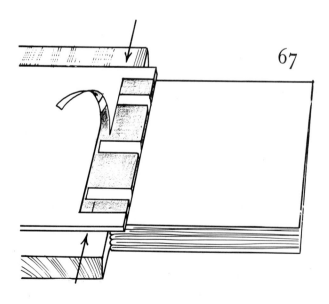

6. ATTACHING BOARDS

With this stage in binding the work begins to assume the appearance of a book. The ends of the tapes, and the mull, are pasted to the inside of both cover boards to make a secure attachment. The backbone board, however, is not made a part of the binding until it is time for the cover material to be attached.

Lay the sewn signatures face up on the bench. Cut two pieces of waxed paper slightly larger than the page of the book. Lay both of these over the first signature and pushed up snug against the hinge, with the tapes *under* the waxed paper, and the mull *above* [FIG. 63]. Smooth the mull down over the waxed paper, and brush paste well into its top surface. If necessary, paste the mull once and let it stand; then paste again [FIG. 64]. Remove and discard the top sheet of waxed paper. Lay the cover board down in position, and check all three sides to see that there is a uniform square all around. Now put the book under weights for a half hour. Remove book from weights, open the board gently and lay it back on a blank board. Using a clean rubbing sheet laid over the mull, rub it down until it is thoroughly dry [FIG. 65].

To paste down the tapes, remove the waxed paper and replace it with a clean sheet. Lay the tapes down on top of the waxed paper and paste them well [FIG. 66]. Two applications may be needed, as the tapes will absorb more paste than the paper will. Now lay all the pasted tapes over on top of the mull, and make sure they are at right angles to the backbone of the book. Discard the soiled waxed paper, and place a clean piece over the first signature. Close the cover of the book. Press down all along the hinge of the cover to stick the tapes. After a few minutes, carefully open the cover to make sure the tapes lie on the inside of the board at right angles. Then close up the cover again and put the work under weights for an hour.

Take the book from weights, open the cover onto a supporting board and inspect the work. The tapes should meet the edge of the mull. If they do not, both the mull and tapes may be trimmed off to a uniform width with the ruler and knife [FIG. 67]. Make light knife cuts. Cut through the tapes and mull only; do not cut into the board. Peel off the waste, and iron down the new edge with the flat folder. Finally, place clean waxed paper inside the cover, close it up, and turn the book over. Proceed to attach the back cover board, following this same procedure. This completes attaching the boards.

7. COVERING

Accuracy and neatness are required in all binding steps, but covering especially demands great care. Considering that the cover material will be turned under the inside edges of both cover boards, it is clear that careful measuring and cutting are required to insure a good job. And since cover paper or cloth is easily stained, extreme care should be used in pasting them. Have plenty of waste newspaper sheets and waxed paper ready for this step. This section will describe covering the boards with paper, but the procedure is the same for cloth.

Select a sheet of cover paper large enough for the entire binding: one piece will cover both the cover boards and the backbone. Lay the paper wrong-side-up on the bench. Using the steel square and a 2H pencil, mark out guide lines for the *corners* of all three boards, as illustrated [FIG. 68]. Allow a ½-inch turnover on all four sides and, of course, the thickness of two boards for each hinge. The amount of turnover should be four times the thickness of the board used.

Transfer measurements directly from the book itself to this cutting layout; even though the boards should be square, it is safest to work from the finished boards themselves. The chief reason for this is that the paper which turns over the edges of the boards cannot be trimmed to size afterwards: it must be tailored at the time it is cut to a uniform width all around. Cut out the cover paper using the square and knife.

Lay the cover paper, wrong-side-up, on a sheet of wastepaper. Lay the backbone board on wastepaper, and brush it well with paste. Discard the wastepaper, then lay the backbone board, paste-side-down, in its proper position on the cover paper. Be precise about registering the board with the corner marks. Rub it down firmly, then turn the work over, and gently mould the cover paper over the edges of the backbone board [FIG. 69].

Turn the work over, wrong-side-up, on a clean waste sheet, with the top edge away from you. This places the work in position for pasting the front cover first. Brush paste over the inside front part of the cover paper, letting the paste run out into the turnover a little. Paste from the center toward the outside edges. Pick up the book and lay it down on the pasted paper, so the front board is in contact with the paste. Be sure the corners of the board line up exactly with the four corner marks [FIG. 70]. Now turn the work over. Place a clean rubbing sheet over the entire front cover, and rub until it is dry, working from the center toward the edges to force out any air bubbles. Then lay the work wrong-side-up again, with the book attached to the left half of the cover paper, and the unattached paper lying flat on the bench. Now brush paste on the inside of the cover paper which is to cover the back cover board. Again,

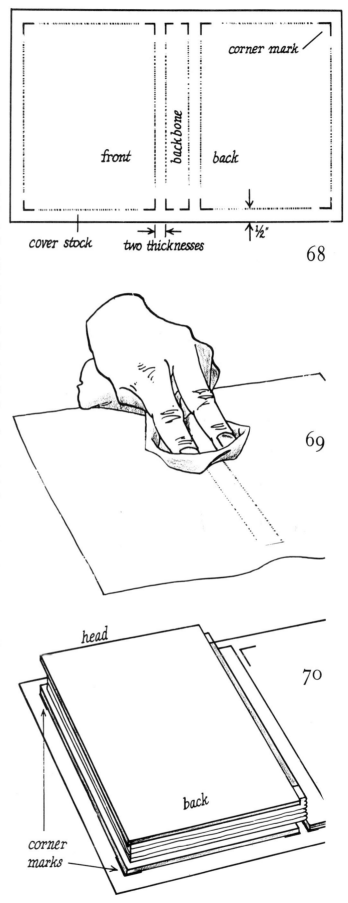

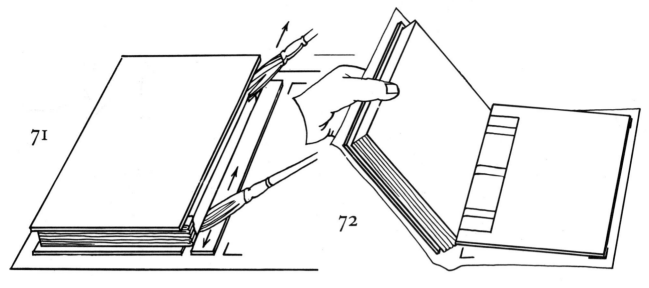

71

72

73

74

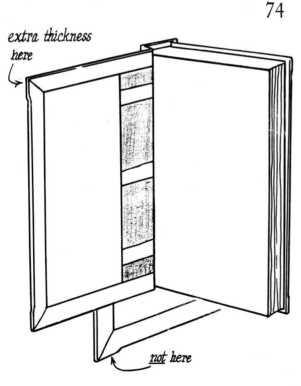

extra thickness
here

not here

let the paste run out into the turnover slightly. Lastly, brush paste down along both hinges, but avoid an excessive amount of paste [FIG. 71].

With the left hand, tip the book up and let the back cover board drop down until it meets the two outside corner marks [FIG. 72]. With the fingers of the right hand, pinch the cover paper tightly into contact with the edge of the board, then slide the hand under the board to finish sticking the paper to it. Place a clean sheet of waxed paper between the board and the signature of the book, close the cover and rub down the paper on the back cover board. Gently mould the edges of the cover paper over the edges of the board. To work the pasted paper down into the hinges, hold the folding stick inside a clean cloth, and run its edge carefully up and down each hinge to form a neat trough [FIG. 73]. Cover both sides of the book with waxed paper and put under weights for a half hour.

The final stage of covering includes mitering the corners of the cover paper and turning in the head and foot, as well as turning in all four sides. This work—described in paragraph eight—should follow without delay, so that after all edges have been turned in a final moulding of the paper in the hinges can be done while the pasted paper is still slightly damp.

8. MITERING CORNERS

Mitering permits the extra fullness of paper to be neatly finished where it turns under at the corner of a board. As these corners are very conspicuous in the finished book, they should be done as expertly as possible. Mitering turns under all the raw edges of the cover material, whether paper or cloth. This prevents cloth from raveling, and in every case makes a more attractive finish. The turnover of the head and foot is done first and the fore-edges last, to keep the single thickness of material at the lower corners, where the greatest wear takes place [FIG. 74].

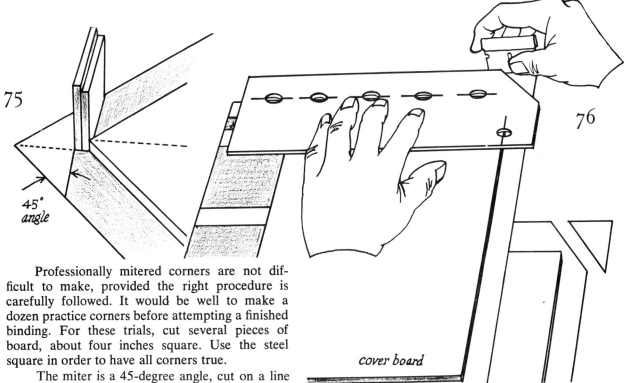

75

**45°
angle**

76

cover board

Professionally mitered corners are not difficult to make, provided the right procedure is carefully followed. It would be well to make a dozen practice corners before attempting a finished binding. For these trials, cut several pieces of board, about four inches square. Use the steel square in order to have all corners true.

The miter is a 45-degree angle, cut on a line beyond the corner of the cover board, and at least the thickness of two boards from it [FIG. 75]. This provides enough extra material to make a lapped joint with the raw edges turned under. It is then clear that the angle on which the cover paper is cut must be accurate, if the finished miter on the inside of the board is to be an accurate 45-degree angle. Each corner to be cut could be marked separately, but a simple jig can be made which will produce perfect results without laborious measuring. (See Part 5, Making Tools and Equipment.)

In the preceding section, we had progressed to the point where the cover paper had been attached but not turned under around the edges. The mitering is done at this point.

Lay the book face down on the bench, and open the back cover to the right onto a supporting board covered with a piece of cardboard. Lay the mitering jig in place on the upper right corner of the board. Line up the edges of the cover board through the holes in the jig [FIG. 76]. Hold the jig down firmly with the left hand, and make the 45-degree cut along the bevel of the jig. Be sure the knife is very sharp. With the cardboard over the supporting board, turn the book and cut miters on the other three corners in the same way. Note that in making the mitering jig, the amount of thickness taken into account depends on the thickness of the cover board. In other words, a separate jig should be made for each thickness of binder's board, and marked accordingly.

In pasting down the turnovers, the head and foot are done first. Stand the book on its backbone on a sheet of wastepaper. With the narrow paste

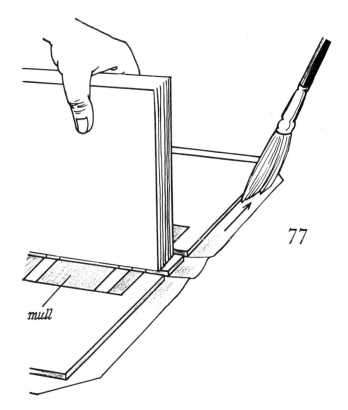

77

mull

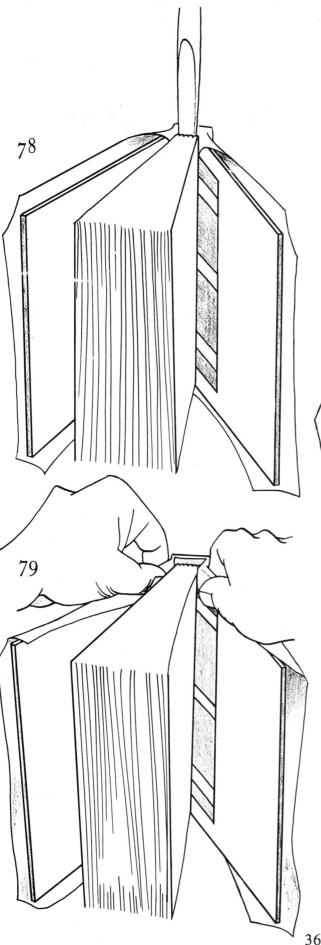

78

79

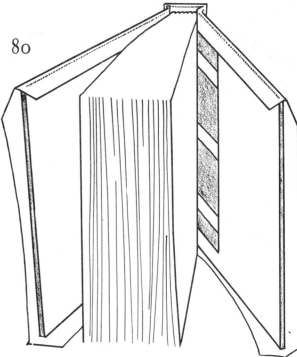

80

brush, paste the turnover clear across the top edge [FIG. 77]. Discard the soiled wastepaper. Stand the book up, with the fore-edges toward you. Using the end of the folding stick, tuck in the pasted turnover down behind the backs of the signatures [FIG. 78]. This may appear very difficult, but it is made easier by using both thumbs in a rolling motion, which helps slide the pasted paper down inside the backbone [FIG. 79]. Continue turning over the paper along the top edges, using this same thumb action. Then lay the book flat on the bench and rub the turnover down well, using a clean cloth [FIG. 80]. Now turn the book end-for-end and follow this same procedure for turning over the paper at the foot.

With both the head and foot turnovers com-

pleted, lay the closed book on the bench and again mould the paper down into the hinges, especially near the head and foot, as illustrated [FIG. 73]. Next, turn over the fore-edges as follows: open the back cover and lay it on a blank board which has been covered with wastepaper. With the small brush, paste lightly inside the pocket of one corner [FIG. 81]. Iron this fold down with the folding needle to make a neat crease against the edge of the board [FIG. 82]. With the same brush, paste the corner of the miter before turning this edge over to form a hem [FIG 83]. Pick up the corner of the miter with the folding needle [FIG. 84], and then fold it over to make a hem of uniform width [FIG. 85]. Iron the hem down flat with the folding needle [FIG. 86]. Prepare the other corner in the same way. Now, brush paste along the whole turn-

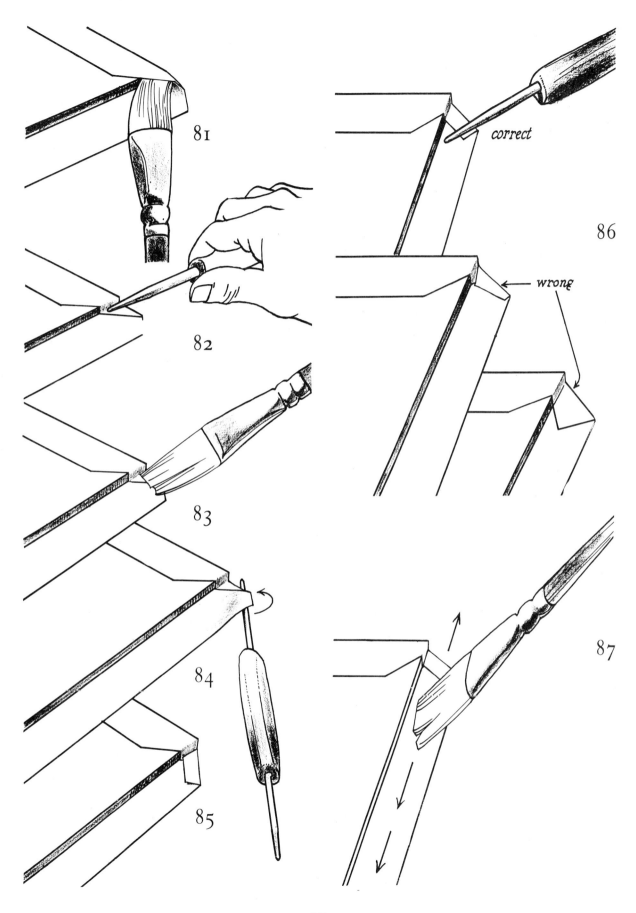

81

82

83

84

85

86

correct

wrong

87

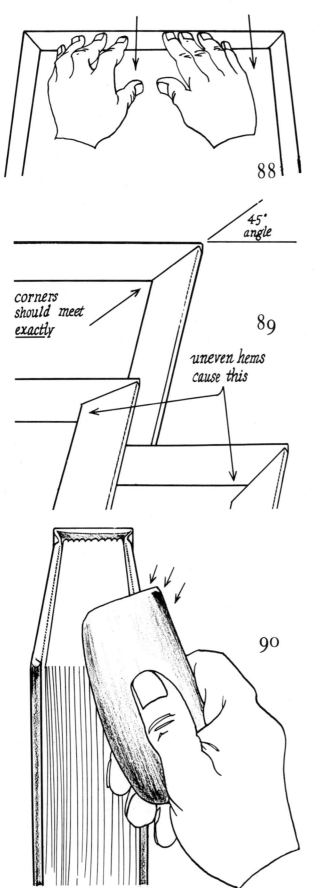

88

45° angle

corners should meet exactly

89

uneven hems cause this

90

over. Do not use an excessive amount, or a lumpy edge will result [FIG. 87]. Remove the soiled wastepaper from under the cover, and draw the turnover up over the edge of the board [FIG. 88]. Pull it back snug against the edge of the board, and rub it down until dry, using a clean cloth. The finished miter should be an accurate 45-degree angle [FIG. 89]. With the flat side of the folder, blunt the corner slightly [FIG. 90], and give the inside of the mitered corner a final ironing to make sure the edges are stuck fast. Turn in the fore-edge of the front cover according to this same procedure. Protect the book with clean pieces of waxed paper and put under weights overnight.

9. PASTING DOWN END SHEETS

This is the final step in the basic construction of a binding. The first leaf of the book, and the last one, are pasted to the inside of the front and back covers, thus covering the mull and tapes, as well as the raw inside surfaces of the boards. Although this may seem to be simply a finishing operation, pasting down the end sheets further reinforces the hinges of the binding.

Lay the book face up on the bench, with the front cover opened and supported by a blank board. Now, turn the first leaf of the book over onto the board, and smooth it out [FIG. 91]. If the foregoing work has been accurately done, there should be a uniform margin around the three sides of the end sheet, and its two corners should exactly strike the joints of the miters. It is not practical to correct a serious fault in these margins, but a limited amount of trimming can be done on the fore-edge of the end sheet. Place a piece of cardboard under the end sheet, and trim with a sharp knife held against the steel-edge ruler [FIG. 92].

Paste down the end sheets as follows: lay the book face-up on the bench. Place two sheets of waxed paper under the end sheet. The top sheet of waxed paper will be used during pasting, while the lower one will stay in place for pressing. Be sure both pieces are pushed well up against the hinge [FIG. 93]. Brush a thin, even coat of paste on the end sheet, starting in the center next to the hinge and working toward the edges. Just before removing the soiled waste sheet, lightly brush paste along the hinge again. Lift the pasted end sheet, and remove the soiled waxed paper. Leave the clean one in place. With the right hand, keep some tension on the lifted end sheet as you carefully close the cover [FIG. 94]. Press the cover in place for an instant, then immediately open the cover and lay it back again on the supporting board. If there are any air bubbles under the end sheet, lift one corner of it, work the air out, then press it back down. Put a clean rubbing sheet over the work,

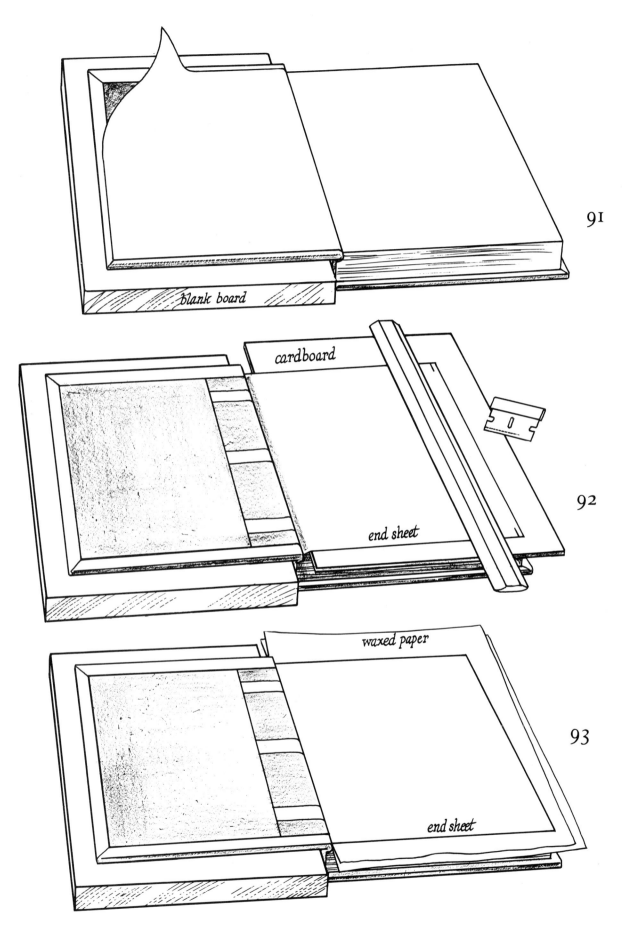

91

blank board

cardboard

end sheet

92

waxed paper

93

end sheet

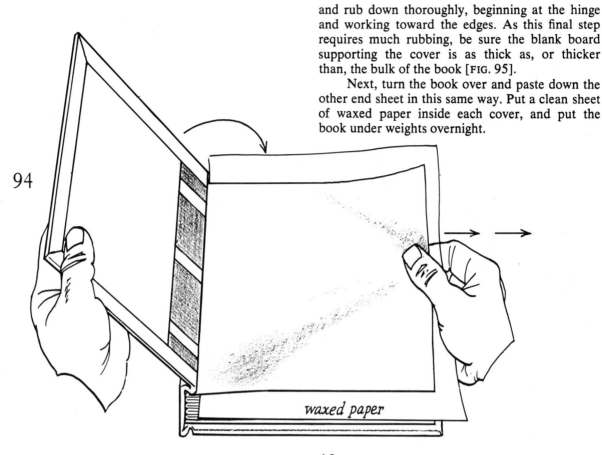

and rub down thoroughly, beginning at the hinge and working toward the edges. As this final step requires much rubbing, be sure the blank board supporting the cover is as thick as, or thicker than, the bulk of the book [FIG. 95].

Next, turn the book over and paste down the other end sheet in this same way. Put a clean sheet of waxed paper inside each cover, and put the book under weights overnight.

94

waxed paper

95

10. LINING THE BOARDS

Attaching decorative lining papers to the insides of the boards is usually considered along with the other refinements in bookbinding. But since it involves the same basic method just described, it is included here. This extra lining paper is often used to obtain additional counter pull, for example when the boards have been covered with a very heavy cloth.

The end sheets are first pasted down in the usual manner, except that they must first be trimmed to fit inside the area bordered by the turnover on all three sides. To locate the lines for trimming, lay the end sheet down smooth against the inside of the cover board. Using the thumb, iron along all three edges to form a crease where the paper laps over the turnover [FIG. 96]. Then place a sheet of cardboard under the end sheet, and cut the three edges back to these lines, Note that a bevel must be cut at the head and foot edges, as illustrated [FIG. 97].

Cut the lining papers to the same size as the book page, but let them reach to within only ⅛ inch of the hinges. Paste and attach the lining papers, making sure that the margin is uniform all the way around [FIG. 98]. Cover the lining paper with a rubbing sheet, and rub down until dry.

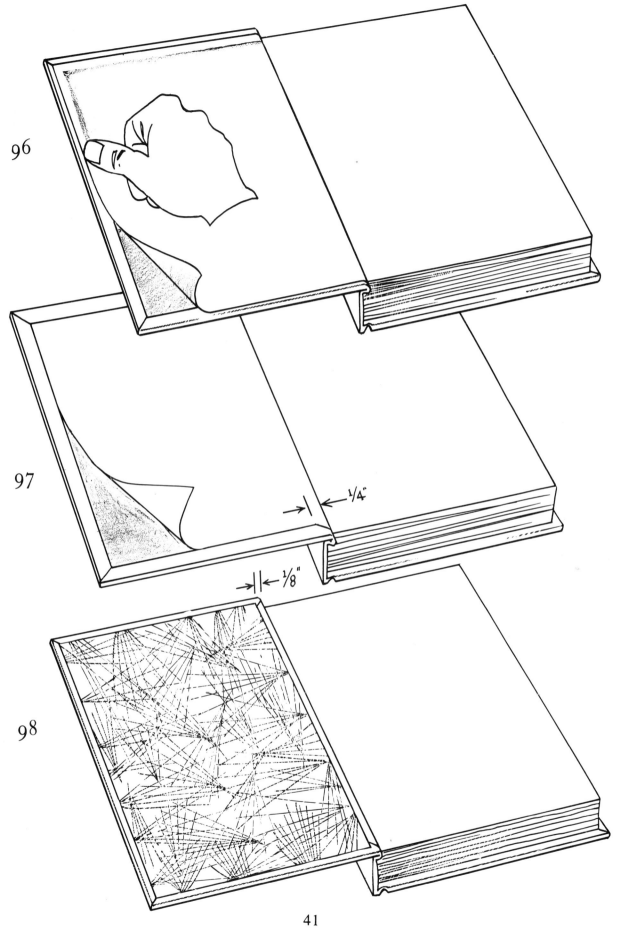

96

97

¼"

⅛"

98

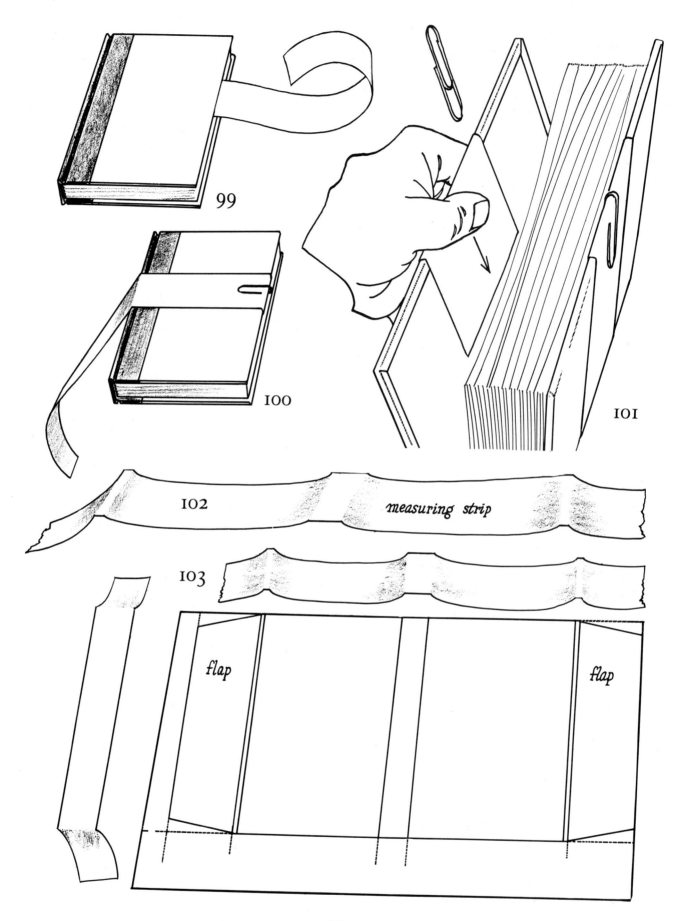

99

100

101

102

measuring strip

103

flap

flap

PART 3

Binding Projects

THE DETAILED METHODS AND PROCEDURES common to all bookbinding have been set forth in the preceding pages. They establish a basic training in the five principal stages of binding, the function and handling of the tools, the proper manipulation of binding materials, and the satisfactory performance of the fundamental steps. With this information as a reference background, the present section describes seven typical binding projects designed to put into practice these basic bookbinding methods.

The description of each binding project begins with an outline of the steps necessary for its completion. When variations or modifications of these steps are introduced, full detailed explanations are given. However, in the case of a commonly repeated step, as, for example, mitering corners, detailed instruction has not been repeated. For any particularly intricate step, consult the foregoing chapters for a complete review.

1. DUST JACKET:

COLORED COVER STOCK, LABEL
ORDER OF WORK:
Select paper
Measure book
Lay out dimensions on paper
Cut and score for folding
Fold up
Make and attach label
Press

A dust jacket serves the dual purpose of providing an attractive wrapper for a book and protecting its covers from dirt and dust. Newly bound books, first editions, or volumes of special value will retain their prime condition longer with this outer protective covering.

Select a paper whose weight, color, and texture are appropriate to the style of the binding to be jacketed. Medium weight paper is the best. Light papers tend to tear at the edges or buckle with changes in the weather. Very heavy papers, on the other hand, are not suited to good clean folds at the hinges and fore-edge, as a result of which the jacket flaps may cause the book covers to pop open. Art supply stores stock a good selection of colored cover papers; and the heavier imported handmade binding papers offer attractive choices of pattern and color.

Measure the book's dimensions with a strip of white wastepaper about two inches wide and long enough to reach completely around the book with four or five inches to spare. Tuck one end of the strip inside the front cover board [FIG. 99]. Fold it around the edge of the cover, and secure this fold with a paper clip [FIG. 100]. Take the paper strip around the backbone and across the back cover, tucking the end inside the back cover. With the thumb, stretch this flap taut, and secure it with another paper clip [FIG. 101]. Run the fingers along all folds where the paper strip goes around the edges of the boards and hinges. Now, remove the strip from the book. It should have six separate creases, from which exact measurements may be obtained [FIG. 102]. Next, using the same method, measure the height of the book. The dust jacket should extend from the head to the foot, without any overhang.

Lay out a cutting diagram on the sheet of cover paper. With the paper right-side-up on the bench, transfer the measurements from the paper strips to the cutting diagram, using the steel square and a sharp 2H pencil to draw light lines of indication [FIG. 103]. The pencil lines will be erased later. Allow for flaps—about one third the width of the covers—which will be folded inside the cover boards. On a small volume make these flaps wider to prevent the covers from popping open [FIG. 104]. The head and foot of the flaps should be beveled, as indicated in the illustration [FIG. 105].

Lay the marked-out cover paper on the cutting section of the bench, and cut it out. Again use the steel square and a sharp knife. Lay the short side of the square even with one long edge of the diagram and in line with the edge of one flap. Make all cuts with one or two light strokes rather than a single heavy one. All vertical cuts should be done with the square; the bevel cuts may be made with the ruler laid in line with pencil guide marks.

Scoring, which is the creasing of a line to be folded, is accomplished by running a blunt-pointed tool across the paper. This compresses the paper

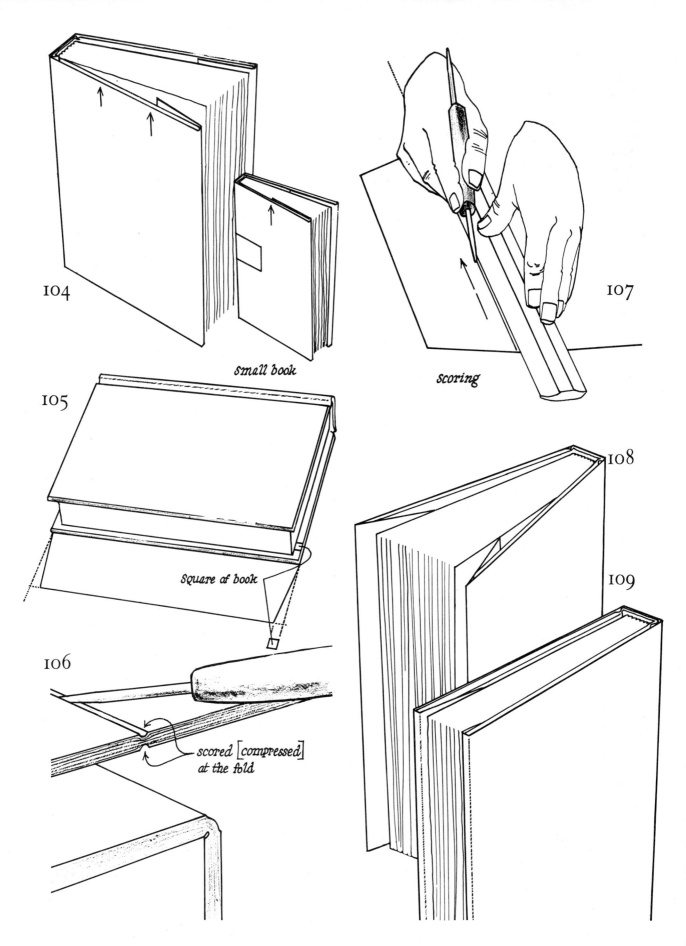

104

small book

105

Square of book

106

scored [compressed]
at the fold

107

scoring

108

109

44

at the folding point, and makes a neat crease without any ragged edge [FIG. 106]. All scoring should be done on the wrong side of the jacket. Therefore, the dimensions should be marked in pencil, using the same paper strip for measurements. Then, lining up the steel-edge ruler with each mark in turn, score the paper with the end of the folding needle. Use a medium pressure: too much may actually cut through the paper [FIG. 107]. Score all six lines in this way. If the folds along the fore-edges are scored only once, the jacket will not close flat [FIG. 108]; a double fold permits a compact, snug fitting jacket [FIG. 109].

Now fold up the jacket. Use the ruler as a folding guide, holding it firmly in line with the scored line. With the right hand, gently fold the paper up against the edge of the ruler [FIG. 110]. Fold each line individually, but do not fold it completely over into a tight crease. This tends to crackle the edge of the fold.

Clean off all pencil guide lines with an Artgum eraser.

Make and attach the label (see Making Labels, p. 83).

Fit the dust jacket to the book, cover it with waxed paper, and put under weights until the label is dry.

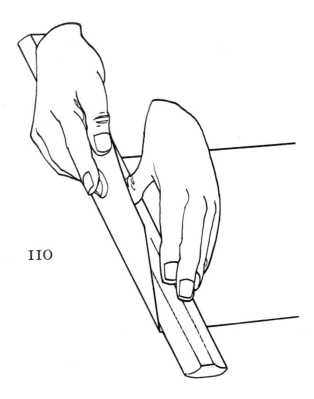

110

2. SINGLE SIGNATURE BOOK:
PAPER COVERS, SEWN AND TIED

ORDER OF WORK:
> Cut and fold signature paper
> Cut cover paper
> Collate
> Mark up and sew
> Fold up cover
> Make and attach label
> Press

A single signature binding of this type makes an attractive notebook, telephone record book, guest book, or one of many similarly useful blank books for the office or home.

Select signature paper and test it for "grain." In order for the leaves of the book to turn nicely, it is preferable to cut the paper so that the fold will run in the same direction as the grain of the paper. To test the paper, place a sheet on the bench and gently roll it back on itself. If the sheet droops down flat, the grain runs parallel to the rolled edge. If the sheet arches up, the grain runs at right angles to the roll [FIG. 111]. Cut six sheets 9 by 12 inches. They are to be folded into a 6 by 9 inch signature. Use the steel square and measure accurately.

Fold the entire signature as one unit. Pick up all six sheets, and tap their top edges gently on the bench. Fold and make a snug crease with the

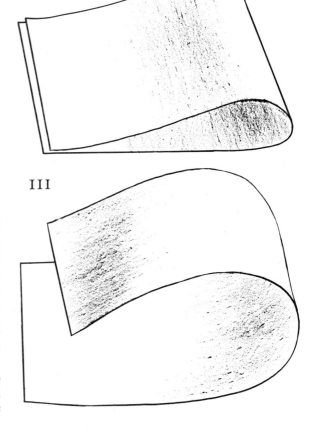

111

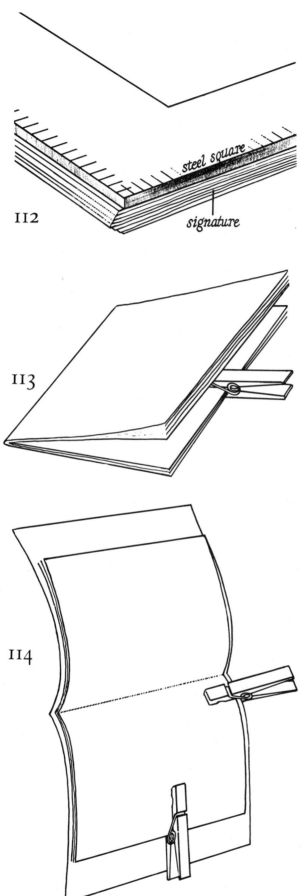

112

113

114

steel square

signature

flat folder. Lay the folded signature on the cutting section of the bench, with the head away from you, and trim the fore-edge as follows: line up the square with the top edges of the signature, and trim off the "V" formed by the edges of the signature paper [FIG. 112]. Use a sharp knife held firmly against the edge of the square. Make several light cuts. After trimming, clip a wooden clothespin over the back half of the signature to hold the alignment, and lay the finished signature aside [FIG. 113].

Next, cut the covers from a single sheet of medium weight cover paper. Allow a square of ⅛ inch along the top edge and the foot. Allow for a 2½-inch flap to fold over the front end sheet, and a similar flap for the back. On the right side of the cover paper lay out a cutting diagram, using the square and light pencil marks. Cut out the cover. Then turn the work over, wrong-side-up, and make a *double* score where the cover folds along the backbone. This is to accommodate the thickness of the signature. Score with the folding needle, then fold the cover along these two lines. Do not fold up the flaps; they will be folded after the sewing is finished.

Collate the book; lay the folded signature inside the folded covers, adjusting it so the square is uniform at the head and foot. Now, clip another clothespin over both the signature and the cover, placing it at the top edge of the back half of the book. This will hold the work in correct alignment for sewing [FIG. 114].

Marking up may be done with the work lying flat on the bench, but the use of the punch board simplifies this step on a book of this kind (see Punch Board, p. 89). Pick up the signature and covers, with the clothespin attached, and place them over the punch board, half the signature on either side of the board [FIG. 115]. Make a pencil mark at the center of the signature, and one mark two inches down from the head; make a third mark two inches up from the foot. With a small awl punch the three holes. Leave the clothespin on the work to hold the alignment [FIG. 116].

Wax a length of thread, then tie a knot in one end leaving a four-inch tail. Thread this on a needle. Remove the work from the punch board and lay it flat on the platform of the sewing frame with the foot toward you. Open the book at the center, and keep it open with the right hand laid inside. The signature and covers are sewn together in the same operation. Start sewing at the center hole, passing the needle from the inside to the outside [FIG. 117]. Draw the thread up against the knot. Now, push the needle in at the top hole, and draw the thread through until it is snug [FIG. 118]. The needle is now passed out again through the center hole [FIG. 119]. Finally, take the needle in

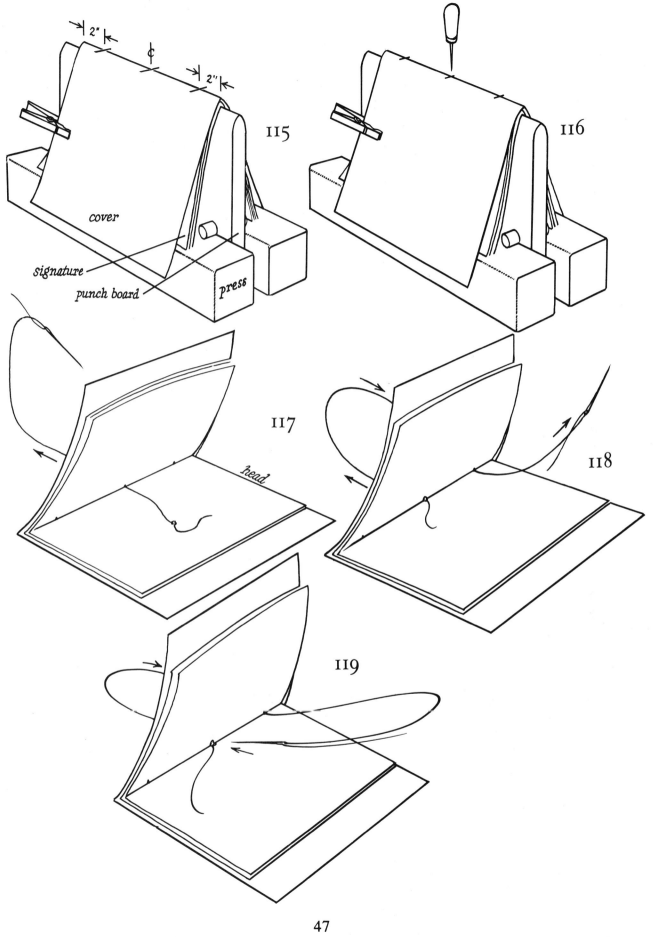

115

cover

signature

punch board

press

116

117

head

118

119

47

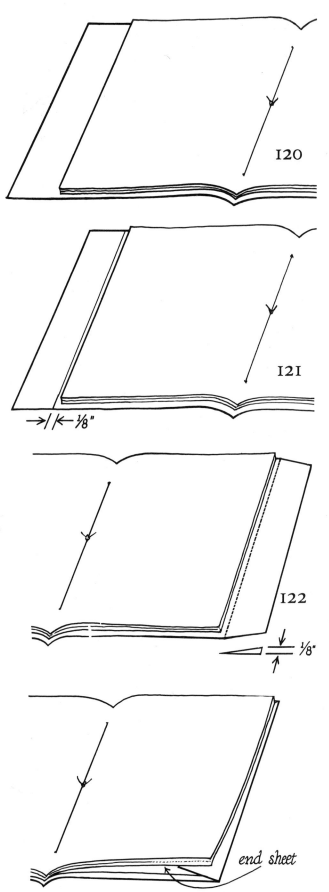

120

121

→| |←⅛"

122

⅛"

end sheet

at the foot hole and draw the thread up snug. Remove the work from the sewing frame, and lay it open flat on the bench. Remove the clothespin. Tie the end of the thread to the knot at the center of the signature, by throwing a loop around *under* the knot, and completing the knot by passing the needle through the loop. Draw the knot up tight, and trim the tails of thread off to within ¼ inch of the knot [FIG. 120].

To fold up the flaps, measure out ⅛ inch beyond the fore-edges of both end sheets, and score for folding [FIG. 121]. Bevel the flaps as illustrated [FIG. 122]. With the ruler as a guide, fold up both flaps, finishing the crease with the flat folder. Slip the front and back end sheets under the corresponding flaps, and close the book.

Make and attach the label (see Making Labels, p. 83).

Put the book under weights until the label is dry.

---

3. FOLIO:

PAPER COVERED BOARDS, FULL LINING

ORDER OF WORK:

      Make boards
      Cut cover paper
      Attach boards
      Miter corners
      Paste down turnovers
      Cut lining paper
      Attach lining
      Make and attach label
      Press

A folio provides a protective case in which to keep frequently used reference materials. For example, a series of type specimen books of the same or similar size are more conveniently stored in a folio than a sewn binding. The individual books can be used separately, and their pages and covers will be protected from damage when put away in the folio. The folio is also ideally suited for the preservation of numerous single items, such as photographs, drawings, letters, or other materials which are either not adapted to sewn binding or which are to be taken out individually.

From medium weight board cut two cover boards 6¼ by 9½ inches. Cut one backbone board ½ by 9½ inches. Round the edges of all three boards, using fine sandpaper held over a sanding block.

From colored or patterned cover stock of your choice, cut a single piece to cover the entire folio. Allow for a ½-inch turnover around all four sides, and the thickness of two boards for each hinge. Place the cover paper wrong-side-up on the bench. Using accurate measurements, lay out a cutting diagram to position each of the three boards.

48

Attach the boards, starting with the front cover. Brush paste onto the wrong side of the paper, letting the paste extend slightly beyond the corner marks. Discard the waste sheet, and lay the work on a fresh piece. Place the cover board in position on the pasted paper, making sure that all four corners are correctly registered. Press down on the board, then immediately turn the work over. Lay a clean rubbing sheet over the work, and rub the surface until the paper is firmly attached and free of air bubbles. Rub from the center toward the sides. Cover the work with a sheet of waxed paper, and put it under weights for a half hour. Paste the remaining areas of the cover paper. Lay the backbone board and the back cover board in position and rub dry as before. When the three boards have been attached, put the finished work, flat, under weights until dry.

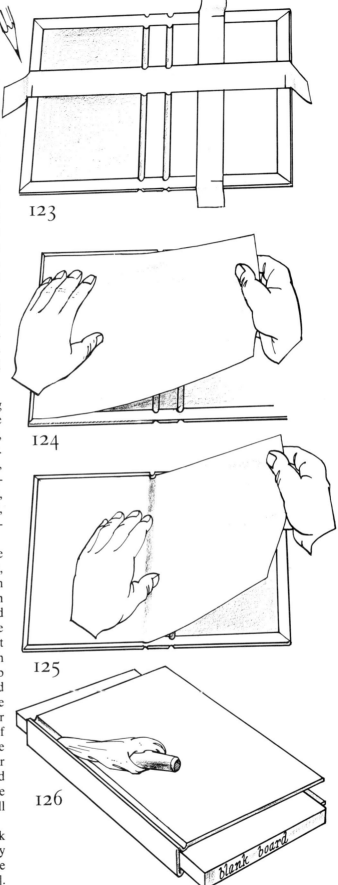

Miter the four corners, using the mitering jig, then paste down the turnovers along the head and foot. Paste and turn over both of the fore-edges. Make sure that all the edges of the turnovers are tightly stuck. Cover the work with waxed paper and put under weights until dry.

Choose an appropriate lining paper, giving some thought to the over-all color scheme. If the boards have been covered with a solid color paper, a decorative lining provides a pleasing contrast. If you have used a patterned paper for the covers, a plain white or buff paper would make an attractive finish inside. In cutting the lining paper, use strips of waste paper, as previously described, to obtain precise measurements. Leave a 3/16-inch margin around all four sides [FIG. 123].

To attach the lining, brush paste on the wrong side of the entire sheet of lining paper, brushing from the center toward the edges. Then pick up the lining paper and lay it in position on the inside of the front (left-hand) cover board [FIG. 124]. Gently rub the left-hand edge of the lining paper down so it will not slip. With the left hand, brush the paper toward the right, then with a finger work the paper down into the hinge. Keep the rest of the pasted paper held clear of the board with the right hand [FIG. 125]. Then attach the paper to the backbone board, and work the paper down into the other hinge. The remaining part of the lining may now be brushed down onto the inside of the back cover with the left hand. Cover the work with a clean rubbing sheet and thoroughly rub down all surfaces until they are firmly attached, making sure the edges are well stuck.

Close up the folio over a ⅜-inch blank board. While the lining paper is still damp, gently crease in both of the hinges with the edge of the folding stick wrapped in a clean cloth [FIG. 126].

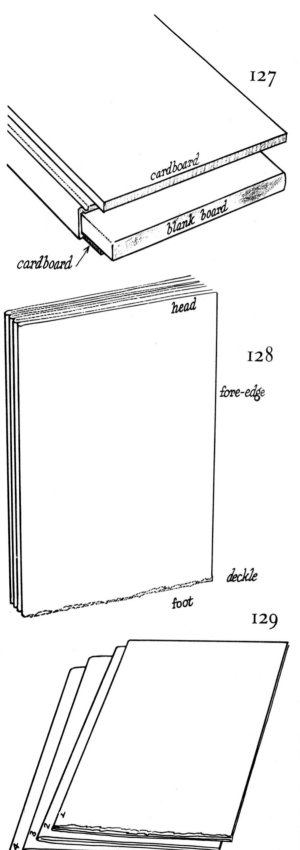

127

128

head

fore-edge

deckle

foot

129

cardboard

blank board

cardboard

Use very light pressure, as the damp paper can easily be torn.

Make and attach the label (see Making Labels, p. 83).

After the label has been attached, place the ⅜-inch blank board inside the folio, and then lay a piece of cardboard on either side of it to protect the hinges from crushing [FIG. 127]. Place the work under weights overnight.

4. BLANK BOOK:

FOUR BLANK SIGNATURES, SQUARE BACK, CLOTH BACKBONE, PAPER SIDES

ORDER OF WORK:

Cut and fold signature paper
Mark up and sew on tapes
Square back and head
Glue up with mull
Make and attach boards
Cover backbone with cloth
Make and attach paper sides
Paste down end sheets
Make and attach label
Press

This binding has many practical uses and because of its solid construction is superior to the commercially made blank books which are marketed as sketch books or notebooks. One of the chief advantages of binding your own blank books is that special papers can be used to suit exactly the purpose of the book. Pen and ink, charcoal, or bond paper may be selected, depending upon the book's function.

Select and test the signature paper for grain. If you plan to use a handmade paper with a *deckle edge,* which is feathered, arrange the cutting so that the deckle will fall at the foot of the folded signature [FIG. 128]. The head edges should be smooth to minimize dust accumulation, and it is usually preferable to have the fore-edges smooth and even as well, to permit easier turning of the leaves.

Cut 16 sheets 9 by 12 inches to be folded up into four signatures of four sheets each, and measuring 6 by 9 inches. Lay the cut sheets on the bench with the heads toward you. Pick up four sheets at a time—enough for one signature—tap the head even, then fold as one unit. Mark this signature with the number "1" next to the fold and near the foot [FIG. 129]. Fold and sign the remaining signatures, following the same procedure.

Gather up the signatures, tap the heads lightly on the bench, then mark up for sewing onto the tapes. Square the back and head with the squared card. Mark up for two ½-inch tapes. Position the tapes so that they balance the weight of the signatures [FIG. 130].

50

Punch the holes, collate, then set up the sewing frame. Wax and knot a piece of thread 24 inches long. This is about the maximum length for convenient sewing. Therefore, on a book of any size, it will be necessary to tie on additional lengths of thread as the sewing progresses. Tie on extra thread in the following way: when the unused thread has diminished to a length of five or six inches, a fresh piece should be tied on. Just after the needle has passed to the outside of a signature, but before it goes over the tape, cut off the thread behind the needle. Tie this loose end to a new length of thread by making a square knot. However, before pulling the knot tight, slip one of the thread ends through the center of the knot. Hold these two ends together while pulling the square knot tight [FIG. 131].

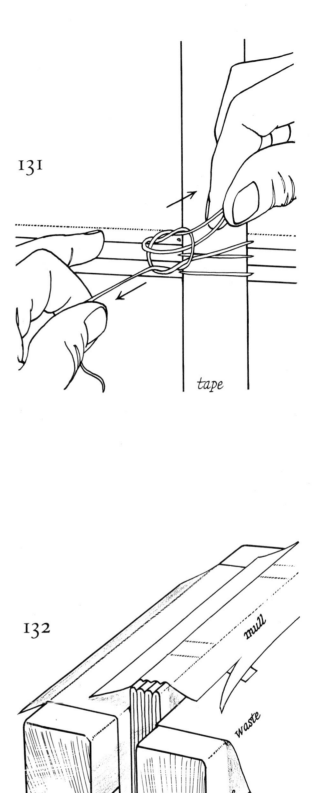

131

tape

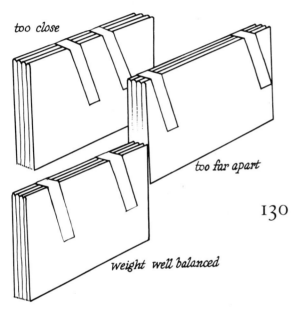

too close

too far apart

130

weight well balanced

This will lock the knot and prevent slipping. Tie the knot as close to the exit hole as possible in order to keep the knot from jamming the next hole.

Sew the signatures onto the tapes. Then paste together the first and second signatures along the hinge, and similarly paste the last two signatures. Put the sewn signatures in the finishing press, making sure they are square across the back and at the head. Tighten up the press, glue up, then attach the mull. Leave the work in the press until it is dry, and then trim the mull and tapes back to within 1½ inches of the hinges [FIG. 132].

Make and attach the boards. There should be a square of ⅛ inch for the boards, and a space the thickness of *two* boards at each hinge. Make the backbone board the same height as the cover boards, and as wide as the combined bulk of the signatures and two boards. After the boards have

132

mull

waste

press

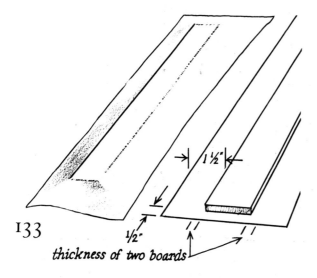

133

thickness of two boards

1½"

½"

been attached, place the book in the finishing press with the backbone projecting about three inches above the face of the press.

In this style of binding, a piece of cloth covers the backbone and extends across the hinges to be attached to the cover boards. Cut a piece of cloth one inch longer than the height of the boards. The width of this cloth should be equal to the total bulk plus the thickness of four boards (two for each hinge), and another three inches to provide for a 1½-inch lap on each cover board. Paste the backbone board and attach it to the wrong side of the cloth. Be sure it is in the proper position [FIG. 133].

To attach the cloth (with backbone board in place), turn the cloth wrong-side-up on a sheet of clean wastepaper, and brush paste onto the cloth on either side of the backbone board. Lay the cloth in place over the backs of the sewn signatures [FIG. 134]. Make sure the top of the backbone board is even with the cover boards. Smooth the cloth down against both cover boards [FIG. 135], and rub down well with a clean cloth.

Take the book out of the press and stand it up on the bench, the fore-edges toward you. Turn in the cloth at the head, using the folding stick. Work it down with the thumbs until it is tight against the edges of the boards [FIG. 136]. Turn the book end-for-end and turn in the cloth at the foot. Put sheets of waxed paper inside both covers, close up the book, then crease the cloth down into both hinges to make neat joints [FIG. 137]. Place the book between pieces of cardboard, and put it under weights until ready for the next step.

Cut two paper panels with which to cover the sides. Each piece should be cut so that the paper laps *over the cloth* ⅛ inch and has the usual ½-inch turnover on the other three sides as well [FIG. 138]. Attach the paper sides, miter the cor-

134

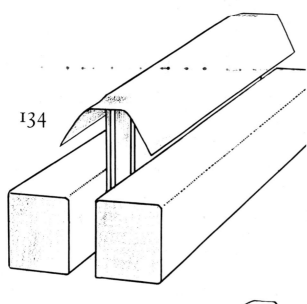

135

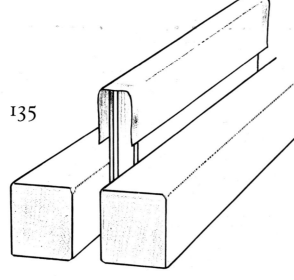

136

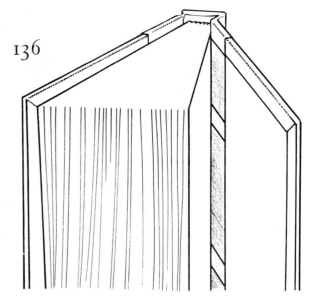

ners, then paste down the end sheets. In all binding, but in this type especially, the appearance of the insides of the boards is important: the mull and tapes should meet on the same line, and the cloth back should turn over in line with the edge of the mull [FIG. 139]. Even though the end sheets cover all of this work, there will remain revealing ridges to tell how well the work was done.

Make a final inspection before putting the book under weights. See that all the edges of the paper are securely pasted, blunt the corners of the boards slightly [FIG. 140], and protect the book with waxed paper.

Finally, make and attach the label (see Making Labels, p. 83).

Press.

A blank book designed for use as a *scrapbook* requires one further step. Since the clippings or other material to be pasted into the scrapbook will add extra thickness to the binding, some provision must be made for this extra bulk. To leave room for this expansion, and thus prevent the binding from bulging open, every other leaf is cut out and removed from the finished binding. This is done as follows: lay the finished blank book on the bench with the backbone to the right. Open the book to the center of the first signature. Lay a piece of cardboard under the left-hand page, making sure the cardboard is pushed up tight against the sewing [FIG. 141]. With the ruler and knife, trim out the page, leaving a "stub" ⅜ inches wide. Remove the cardboard, turn the leaf, then trim out the next leaf in the same way. Proceed to the back of the book, but do not cut any leaves beyond the center of the last signature. The purpose of leaving the stubs is to preserve the sewing intact. *Tearing out* the leaves would, of course, destroy the binding altogether.

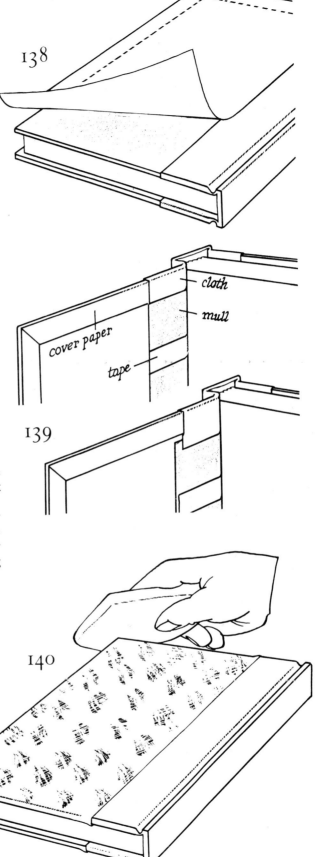

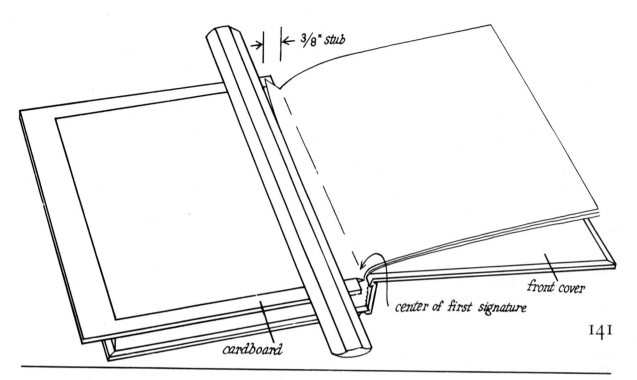

3/8" stub

141

front cover

center of first signature

cardboard

5. MANUSCRIPT BINDING:

SINGLE SIGNATURE, CASE BINDING

ORDER OF WORK:

Guard the sheets
Make end sheets
Collate
Fold signature
Sew on tapes and mull
Trim fore-edge
Make case binding
(directions in project No. 6)

This binding is used when a manuscript made up of numerous single sheets is prepared for sewing as a folded signature. As the single sheets must first be transformed into folded ones, the initial step is the *guarding* of the sheets. Guarding in this case means pasting the sheets up into pairs which may then be folded. (See also p. 59 for guarding of damaged leaves.) This is accomplished by pasting those sheets comprising the front half of the manuscript to the corresponding sheets in the back half, and then folding them as one signature.

Let us assume that a typewritten manuscript is to be bound in this manner. Divide the manuscript into two equal halves. For example, if there are ten sheets, lay the first five sheets *face down* on the bench to the left; then lay the last five sheets *face up* to the right. If the manuscript has an odd number of sheets, add a blank sheet to the front. On each of the sheets which make up the front half of the manuscript make two pencil marks ¼ inch from the back edges: these are guide marks [FIG. 142]. Next, trim ¼ inch from the back edges of all the sheets which make up the back half of the manuscript. To do this, tap the top edges down on the bench to obtain good alignment. Lay the sheets

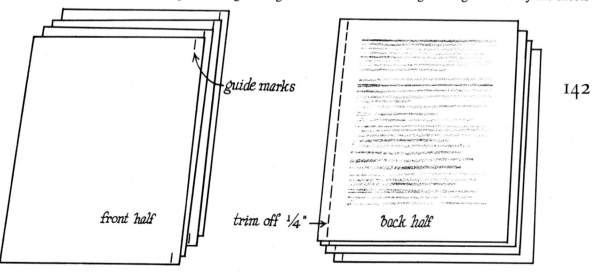

guide marks

front half

trim off ¼"

back half

142

54

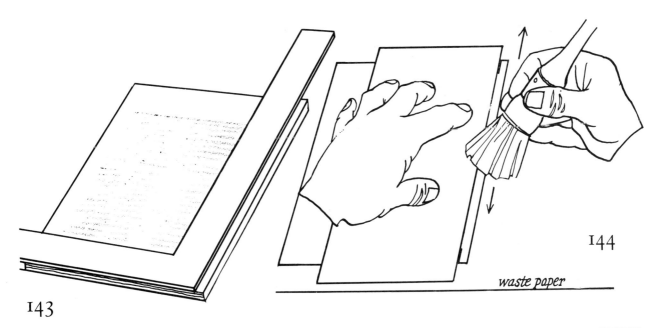

143

144

waste paper

on the bench with the top edges toward you. Place the steel square in line with this top edge, and trim all the sheets at the same time [FIG. 143].

To paste the sheets into pairs, lay the first page of the manuscript face down on wastepaper. Over this, and in line with the guide marks, lay a *straight* piece of wastepaper. Now, brush paste along the exposed edge of the manuscript sheet [FIG. 144]. Pick up the pasted sheet and lay it on clean wastepaper. The *last page of the manuscript* is now attached to this pasted edge—again, in line with the two guide marks. Note that the left-hand page is face down, and the right-hand one face up [FIG. 145]. Lay a clean rubbing sheet over this joint, and rub dry. Then place these joined sheets under weights. Proceed pasting up the remaining pairs of sheets in the same way, until the last two, which form the center of the signature, have been pasted together. As each pair of sheets is completed, put them under weights to dry with the rest. Do not fold up the sheets; the folding is done later.

To provide end sheets for attaching to the boards, as well as blank leaves at the beginning and end of the bound manuscript, new end sheets are now added. Cut three sheets of white bond paper to the same size as the double sheets just pasted together. Leave the fore-edges a little full, as the entire signature is to be trimmed after folding.

Next, collate the work. Take the guarded manuscript sheets from the weights, and verify the order in which they are laid together. Lay them on top of the three new end sheets, with the center pages of the manuscript facing up. Pick up the entire set of sheets and tap the top edges down for alignment [FIG. 146]. Lay them on the bench with the head toward you, and fold them as one signature [FIG. 147].

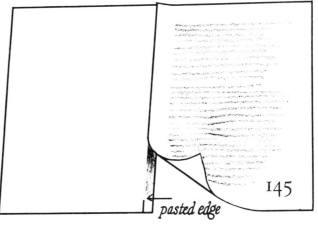

pasted edge

145

146

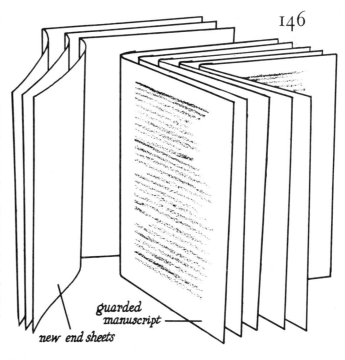

guarded manuscript

new end sheets

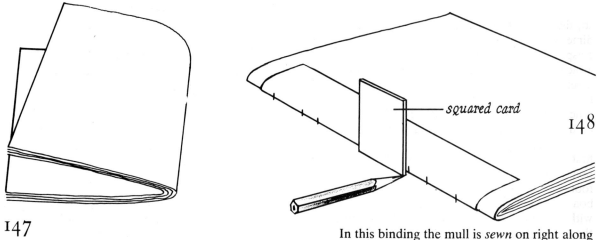

squared card

148

147

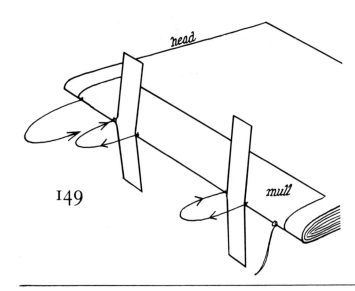

head

149

mull

In this binding the mull is *sewn* on right along with the tapes, rather than being glued up after sewing. Before marking up, cut a piece of linen mull, then fold it lengthwise down the center, creasing it with the flat folder. Slip the creased mull over the back of the signature, and mark up for two ½-inch tapes [FIG. 148]. Wax a length of thread and knot one end, leaving a three-inch tail. Set up the sewing frame and begin sewing at the outside of the foot. Sew in and out all the way to the head, passing the thread over each tape in turn [FIG. 149]. After the needle is drawn out at the head, pull the thread up snug. Then sew back again to the foot. Tie a knot under the starting knot, and trim off the tails to within ¼ inch of the knot.

Finally, trim the fore-edge. Use a sharp knife held firmly against the steel square. Many light cuts produce a cleaner edge.

Place the finished signature under the weights to compress the fold. It is now ready to be attached to the case binding, whose construction is described in the following section.

6. CASE BINDING:

SQUARE BACK, PAPER COVERED BOARDS
ORDER OF WORK:
Make boards
Mark out and cut cover paper
Attach boards
Miter corners
Attach case to signature
Paste down end sheets
Make and attach label
Press

150

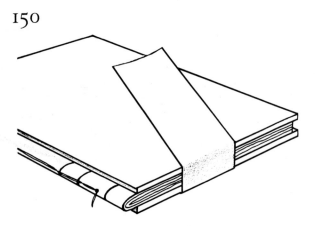

In commercial binding the covers, backbone, and cover material are fabricated as a separate unit quite apart from the sewn signatures of the book itself. Such books are rarely sewn on tapes, but are reinforced with a light muslin mull, which is often called *super*. The mull then becomes the sole means of attaching the book to its case. This obvious lack of strength limits the life of the binding; but the hand bookbinder can correct much of this weakness by sewing the signatures on tapes. Even so, the case binding must be made to the precise dimensions of the book in order for the hinges to clasp the book tightly, and thus provide a secure attachment. In binding a single signature book with a very narrow backbone, the problem of turning in the cover material at the head and foot is very much simplified by the use of a case binding, since all this work is done with the case flat on the bench.

In making a case, therefore, measuring is the first and most critical step. Make the two cover boards first. Allow a square of ⅛ inch at the head, foot, and fore-edge. Allow the thickness of two boards at each hinge. Round the edges of the boards with fine sandpaper, then lay the signature between the boards and measure the total bulk, using a strip of wastepaper [FIG. 150]. This dimension will be the width of the backbone board; it should be the same height as the cover boards. Next, lay the backbone in place against the back of the signature, and hold it in place with a length of gummed tape. With another strip of wastepaper measure all the way around the book. Be sure the strip is forced down into the hinges to obtain an accurate measurement [FIG. 151]. Make creases with the fingers along every edge.

Using these dimensions mark out a cutting diagram on the wrong side of a sheet of cover paper. Use the steel square in conjunction with a sharp 2H pencil to locate the corner marks for all three boards. Attach the boards, then place the case flat under weights to dry.

Miter the four corners, and paste down the turn-overs. Be sure to do the fore-edges last. Close the case over a blank board, and carefully mould the paper down into the hinges. Protect the work with waxed paper, and put under weights until it is dry.

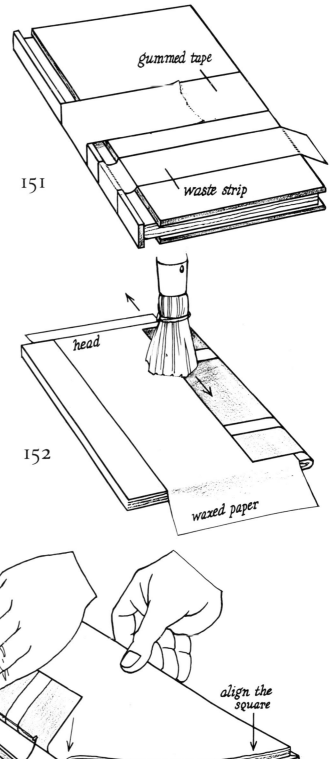

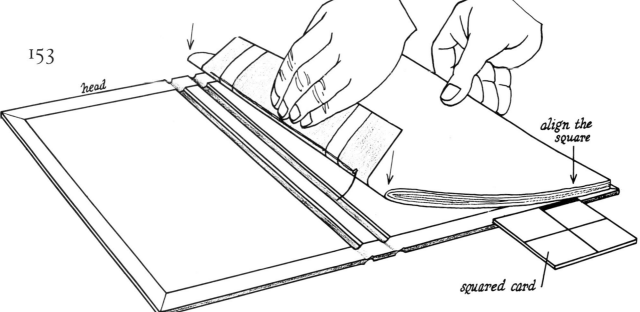

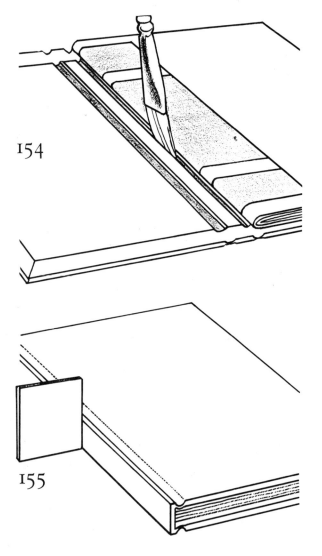

154

155

To attach the case, lay the signature face down on wastepaper. The mull and tapes will be pasted to the *back cover* of the case first. With a sheet of waxed paper under the tapes and mull, brush paste on the mull, then stick the tapes to it. Paste again, working paste well into the tapes [FIG. 152]. Lay the finished case open flat on the bench with the head away from you. Lay the signature in position—with the pasted mull down—on the inside of the back cover board. Hold the unpasted mull in the left hand, lowering the signature into place as you align the square on the three edges of the board [FIG. 153]. With the squared card, check the square carefully, then drop the pasted mull down onto the board. Cover the work with clean wastepaper, and place it under weights for a half hour.

To attach the front half of the case, lay it open flat on the bench with the head away from you. Paste up the front mull as before, then discard the soiled waxed paper. With the narrow paste brush, brush paste lengthwise into both hinges [FIG. 154]. Pick up the front cover, and carefully close it down into contact with the pasted mull. Stand the squared card against the backbone to make sure it is at right angles to the bench [FIG. 155]. Cover the work with wastepaper and place it under weights for a half hour.

Remove the book from the weights, and mould the joints once again, using the edge of the folding stick. Again put the book under weights overnight to dry.

Paste down the end sheets, then put under weights to dry.

Make and attach label. (See Making Labels, p. 83.)

Press.

---

7. SHEET MUSIC:

CLOTH BACK, PAPER SIDES

ORDER OF WORK:

    Guard sheets
    Repair corners
    Make end sheets
    Collate
    Make linen mull
    Mark up and sew
    Make and attach boards
    Cut and attach back cloth
    Cover sides
    Paste down end sheets
    Make and attach label
    Press

Sheet music may be preserved in a binding which will last almost indefinitely. The repeated, hard use of music books causes serious wear and damage, especially along the folded back edge where it was originally sewn or stapled, and at the

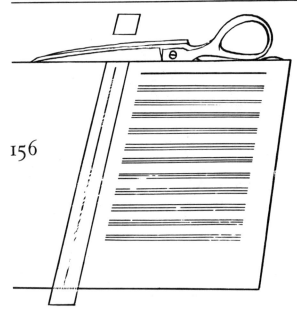

156

top corners, as the result of constant turning of the leaves.

Guarding in this case means the repair of the damaged places, preparatory to sewing the work up as a single signature. If the inside margins of the music are wide enough, thin strips of tough Japanese paper may be used. If mending cannot be done without lapping over the printed music, then transparent mending silk should be used.

First, take the music apart, carefully removing the old metal staples or sewing. As each folded sheet is removed, mark its lower front corner with a signature number for collating. Even though some of the sheets are in better condition than others, it is best to guard them all to make a good binding. Lay the separated sheets face up on the bench.

Cut guard strips ¾ inch wide and about one inch longer than the height of the page. Start with

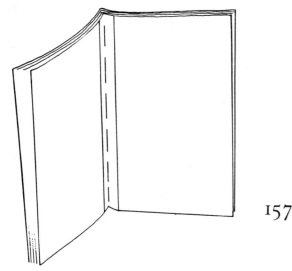

157

158

159

new paper

music

waste paper

the center pages. Lay the center sheet flat on a piece of waste paper. Paste the guard strip and lay it over the center fold of the sheet. Smooth it down onto the sheet music [FIG. 156]. Cover it with a rubbing sheet, and rub it well. Pull the guarded sheet loose from the wastepaper and trim the two ends of the guard strip even with the sheet music, using the shears. Turn the sheet over and guard the back side in the same way. This extra reinforcement of the center sheet provides the necessary backing to hold the sewing. Proceed to guard the remaining sheets in the same way, but on the inside only [FIG. 157].

"Dog-eared" or badly damaged corners may be mended with patches of new paper [FIG. 158]. Select paper as nearly like the original in color and texture as possible. It may be lighter weight, however. Cut a piece of paper large enough to cover the damaged area and reach diagonally across the corner of the page [FIG. 159]. Lay the sheet to be mended on a piece of clean wastepaper. Paste the

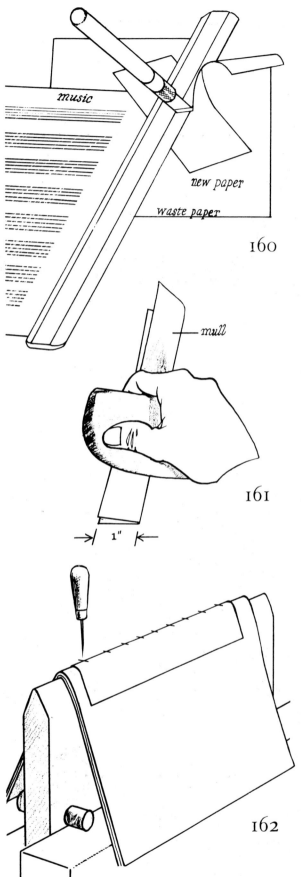

160

161

→| 1" |←

162

patch, then lay it over the damaged corner. Rub it down well, using a clean rubbing sheet. Stick the ends of the patch to the wastepaper as well. Now transfer all the work, including the wastepaper, to the cutting section of the bench. Trim off both sides of the new patch, using the ruler and lining it up accurately with the edges of the page [FIG. 160].

As each folded sheet is guarded and mended, lay it aside, open and face down on the bench. Finally, check the collation.

Make four new end sheets from paper as close to the original as possible. Cut two pieces of paper to be folded to the same size as the music. Do not fold until later. Trim the head and foot edges to the identical dimensions of the sheet music. Now, collate the end sheets with the music, tap all the top edges gently on the bench, then fold up all the sheets as one signature.

Cut a piece of linen mull two inches wide and one inch shorter than the height of the signature. Fold it lengthwise and crease it with the flat folder [FIG. 161]. Lock the punch board in the finishing press. Place the folded signature over the punch board, with one half on either side of it. Then lay the creased mull over the back of the signature, adjusting it so there is a ½-inch margin at the head and foot. As there are no tapes used in this binding, a series of evenly spaced holes is made to receive the sewing. Mark up for punching, with a mark one inch in from the head and another mark one inch in from the foot. Place the other marks so that they are spaced regularly along the backbone approximately an inch apart [FIG. 162]. Now, punch all the holes with a small awl. Clip a clothespin over the head of the signature in order to hold it in alignment with the mull.

Wax a length of thread, and knot one end. Lay the signature on the platform of the sewing frame, and place your right hand inside the center of the signature. Starting at the foot (bottom hole), sew toward the center from the outside, and continue sewing in and out to the head. Draw the thread up tight, then sew in and out again back to the foot. Draw the thread tight, and tie a knot under the starting knot. Trim off the tails to within ¼ inch of the knot [FIG. 163].

The cover boards for sheet music should be made the same height as the leaves of the music. The music must not only lie open easily in a flat position, but it must be possible to turn the pages quickly. The omission of any square, or overhang, assists in turning the pages. However, to insure flexible joints, allow the boards to come within only ¼ inch of the backbone. Attach the boards by the mull, making sure the edges of the boards are even with the fore-edges of the signature [FIG. 164]. Put under weights to dry.

Next, cut a piece of buckram or other cloth

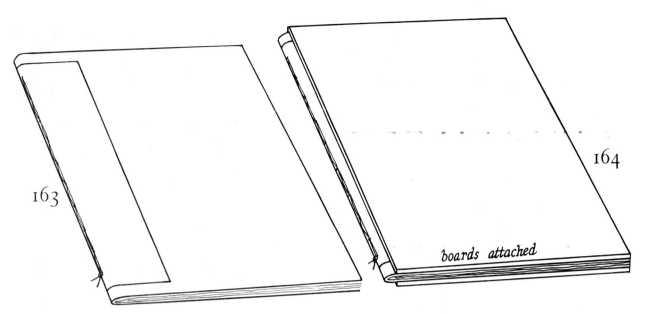

163

164

boards attached

with which to cover the backbone. This cloth back should be three inches wide and one inch longer than the height of the boards to allow for a ½-inch turnover at the head and foot. Place the book between two pieces of cardboard, and put it in the finishing press. Crease the backbone cloth down the center, and brush paste on the wrong side of it. Paste it again, then lay it over the backbone of the book [FIG. 165]. Make sure there is a uniform ½-inch turnover at the head and foot. With the fingers, pinch the cloth into contact with the boards and the projecting back edge of the signature. Using a clean cloth, rub down all surfaces of the cloth until it is well attached. Remove the book from the press, and stand it up with the fore-edge facing you.

165

blank boards

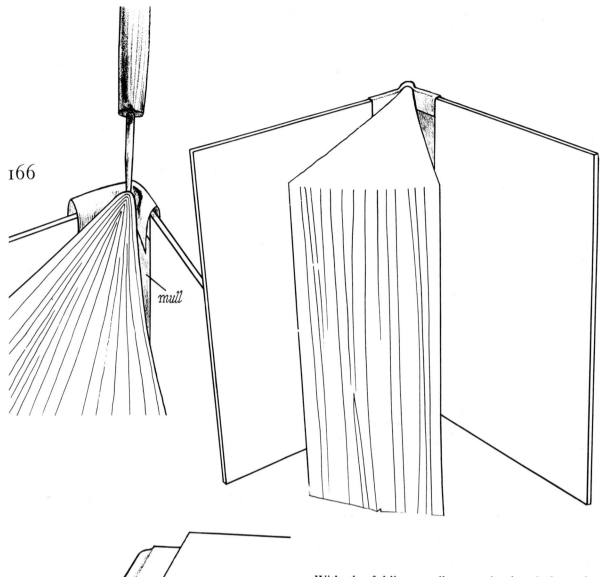

166

mull

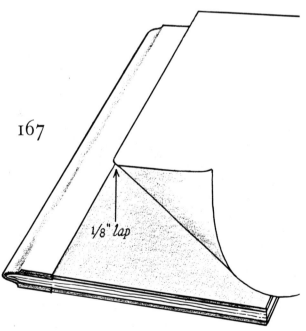

167

1/8" *lap*

With the folding needle, turn in the cloth at the head to form a neat cap. Work the cloth down against the insides of both boards, using the thumbs. This requires some patience because the turnover is actually stuck to itself, and there is very little space available for this turnover [FIG. 166]. Turn the book end-for-end, and turn in the cloth at the foot.

Make and attach paper sides. Allow a ½-inch turnover around the three sides of the boards and ⅛ inch to lap over the edge of the cloth back [FIG. 167]. Rub down all edges of the turnovers, and be sure that the paper is tightly stuck where it laps over the cloth.

Put the book under weights to dry for half an hour.

Then paste down the end sheets.

Make and attach the label (see Making Labels, p. 83).

Press.

PART 4
Advanced Procedures

1. REBINDING AN OLD BOOK

AN IMMEDIATELY PRACTICAL USE OF HAND bookbinding is the repair and preservation of the books in the home library which have worn out, but which are valuable enough to warrant new bindings. Books in this category may have been published either in hard covers (boards) or as paperbacks. In the preceding section the square back binding has been stressed because of its suitability to books with relatively few signatures [FIG. 168]. However, the majority of hardbound trade books have considerably more signatures. As a consequence of their greater bulk, the backs of the sewn signatures are rounded, which offsets this increased thickness, and at the same time forms a convenient shoulder against which the edges of the boards fit [FIG. 169]. The better paperbacks— that is, those originally manufactured as folded and sewn signatures—may also be rebound according to the following procedure. But the cheaper paperbacks—known as "perfect bindings"—are *not* practically suited to rebinding because they are made up of single leaves glued along the backbone with a flexible glue. Originally published at a very low price, they lack the quality of paper which warrants guarding all the single sheets and then sewing them up as signatures.

In the typical hardbound trade book, the cloth covering is attached over a hollow backbone, so that the cloth will conform to the rounded back. The following procedures describe the preparation of such a book for rebinding. They supplement the general procedures already discussed in Parts 2 and 3, which are still to be followed in their proper sequence, as required in the following advanced steps.

A. Tearing Apart

Before an old book can be rebound, its worn covers, mull, and stitching must be removed [FIG. 170). This is called *tearing apart*. The term suggests rough handling, but great care is called for to prevent damaging the signatures. Tearing apart is done in the following way.

Lay the book face up on the bench, and open the front cover. With a sharp knife slit along the hinge, cutting through the old cloth covering and

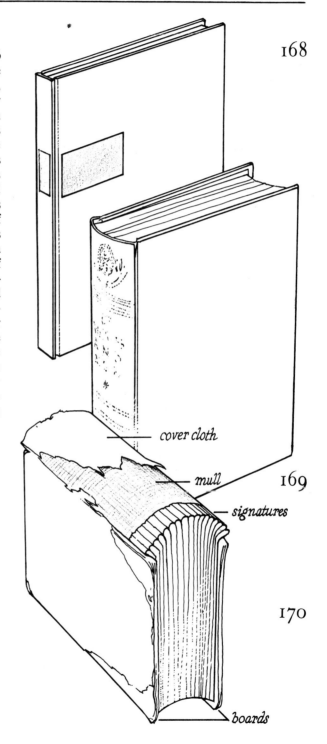

168

cover cloth

mull 169

signatures

170

boards

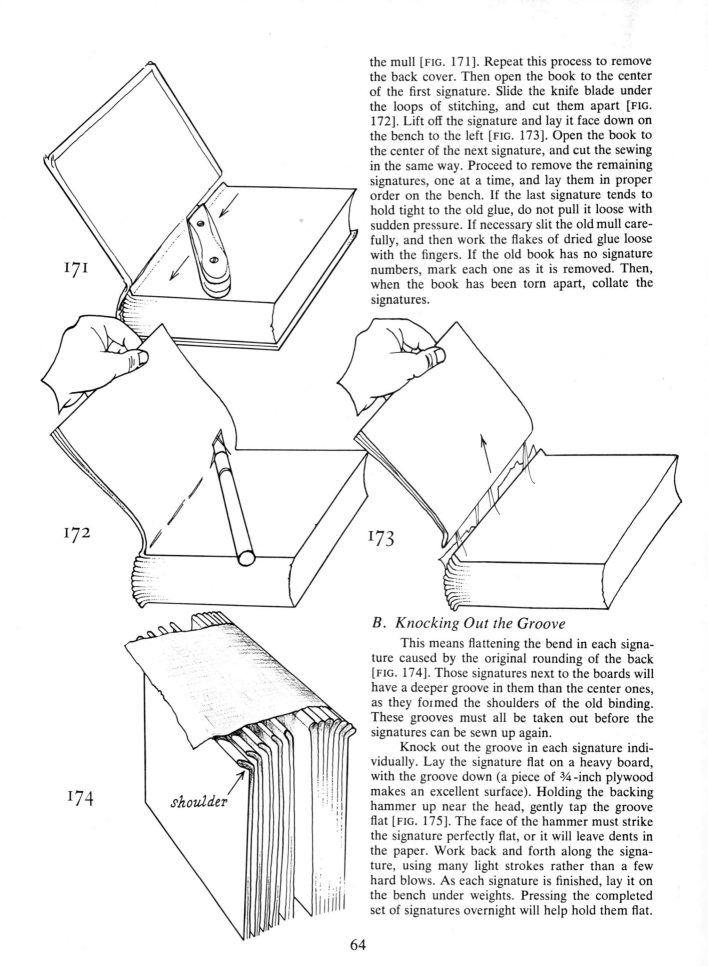

the mull [FIG. 171]. Repeat this process to remove the back cover. Then open the book to the center of the first signature. Slide the knife blade under the loops of stitching, and cut them apart [FIG. 172]. Lift off the signature and lay it face down on the bench to the left [FIG. 173]. Open the book to the center of the next signature, and cut the sewing in the same way. Proceed to remove the remaining signatures, one at a time, and lay them in proper order on the bench. If the last signature tends to hold tight to the old glue, do not pull it loose with sudden pressure. If necessary slit the old mull carefully, and then work the flakes of dried glue loose with the fingers. If the old book has no signature numbers, mark each one as it is removed. Then, when the book has been torn apart, collate the signatures.

171

172

173

174 *shoulder*

B. Knocking Out the Groove

This means flattening the bend in each signature caused by the original rounding of the back [FIG. 174]. Those signatures next to the boards will have a deeper groove in them than the center ones, as they formed the shoulders of the old binding. These grooves must all be taken out before the signatures can be sewn up again.

Knock out the groove in each signature individually. Lay the signature flat on a heavy board, with the groove down (a piece of ¾-inch plywood makes an excellent surface). Holding the backing hammer up near the head, gently tap the groove flat [FIG. 175]. The face of the hammer must strike the signature perfectly flat, or it will leave dents in the paper. Work back and forth along the signature, using many light strokes rather than a few hard blows. As each signature is finished, lay it on the bench under weights. Pressing the completed set of signatures overnight will help hold them flat.

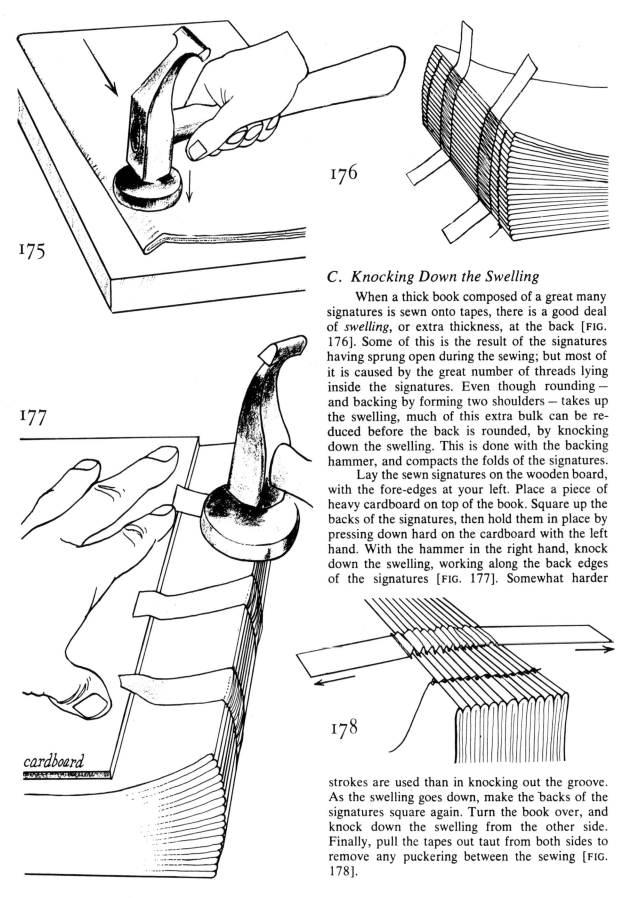

175

176

177

cardboard

178

C. Knocking Down the Swelling

When a thick book composed of a great many signatures is sewn onto tapes, there is a good deal of *swelling*, or extra thickness, at the back [FIG. 176]. Some of this is the result of the signatures having sprung open during the sewing; but most of it is caused by the great number of threads lying inside the signatures. Even though rounding — and backing by forming two shoulders — takes up the swelling, much of this extra bulk can be reduced before the back is rounded, by knocking down the swelling. This is done with the backing hammer, and compacts the folds of the signatures.

Lay the sewn signatures on the wooden board, with the fore-edges at your left. Place a piece of heavy cardboard on top of the book. Square up the backs of the signatures, then hold them in place by pressing down hard on the cardboard with the left hand. With the hammer in the right hand, knock down the swelling, working along the back edges of the signatures [FIG. 177]. Somewhat harder strokes are used than in knocking out the groove. As the swelling goes down, make the backs of the signatures square again. Turn the book over, and knock down the swelling from the other side. Finally, pull the tapes out taut from both sides to remove any puckering between the sewing [FIG. 178].

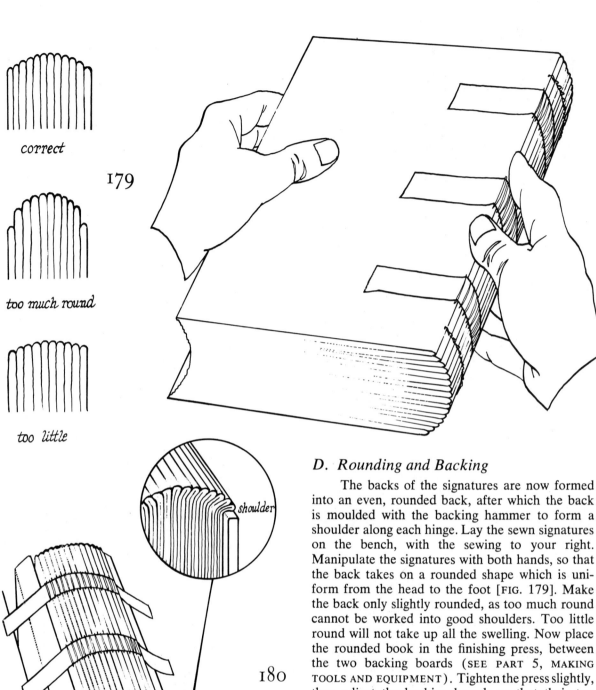

correct

179

too much round

too little

shoulder

180

$\frac{3}{16}''$

D. Rounding and Backing

The backs of the signatures are now formed into an even, rounded back, after which the back is moulded with the backing hammer to form a shoulder along each hinge. Lay the sewn signatures on the bench, with the sewing to your right. Manipulate the signatures with both hands, so that the back takes on a rounded shape which is uniform from the head to the foot [FIG. 179]. Make the back only slightly rounded, as too much round cannot be worked into good shoulders. Too little round will not take up all the swelling. Now place the rounded book in the finishing press, between the two backing boards (SEE PART 5, MAKING TOOLS AND EQUIPMENT). Tighten the press slightly, then adjust the backing boards so that their top edges are about $\frac{3}{16}$ of an inch below the edges of the two outside signatures [FIG. 180]. This will form a shoulder the same width as the thickness of the boards to be used. Check the round of the back again, correcting any irregularities by working the signatures up from under the press. Finally, tighten the press securely.

Now, back the book, using a series of gentle glancing blows of the hammer. The hammer strokes should begin near the center of the back, glancing toward the hinges [FIG. 181]. This process requires patience, and a great many light blows to bend the signatures gradually down onto the beveled edges of the backing boards. The signatures next to the

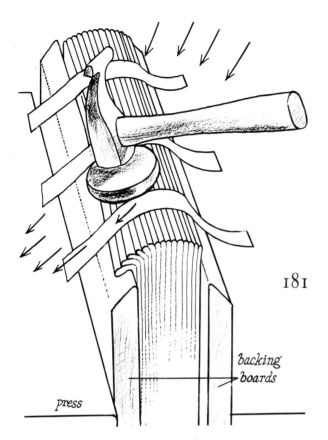

181

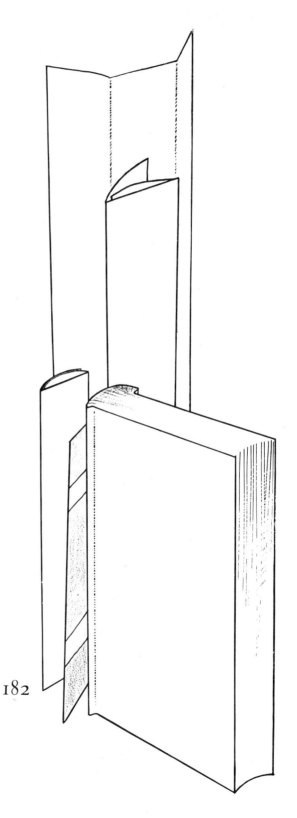

backing boards

press

182

backing boards will have more shoulder than those in the center of the book. Work slowly back and forth along the backs of the signatures until both shoulders are evenly formed. The rounded and backed book may now be glued up and the mull attached while the work is securely locked in the press.

E. Making a Hollow Back

In former times when a large, round backed book with many signatures was covered with leather, the leather was firmly glued directly to the backs of the signatures. But because cloth will not withstand the constant flexing which leather will, modern binding employs a *hollow back*, to which the cloth is glued. This allows the book to open and shut without bending the cloth over the backbone. A hollow back is simply a flat tube made of heavy kraft paper, the same height as the cover boards and three times the width of the backbone. This is folded lengthwise into three panels, then pasted together to form a hollow flat tube. The single thickness of paper is glued to the backs of the signatures, while the double layer is attached to the cloth covering [FIG. 182].

The hollow back is attached over the mull, just before the cloth covering is pasted to the boards.

2. MAKING SPLIT BOARDS

Split boards is a term which describes cover boards made in two layers with the sewing tapes

67

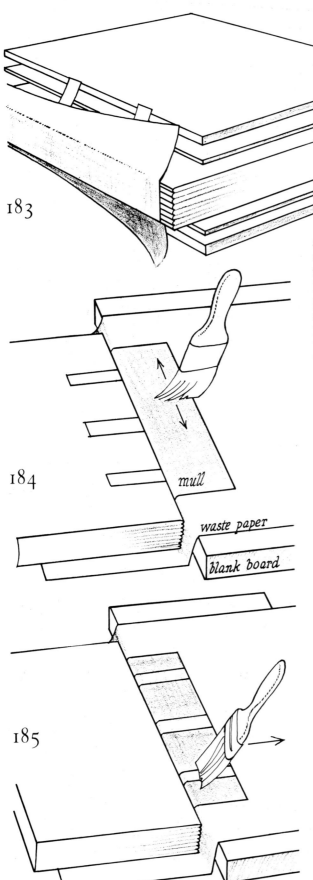

183

don't sand meeting edges

184

mull

waste paper

blank board

185

and mull pasted between them. In this way the mull and tapes become an integral part of the boards, thereby producing the strongest possible binding. Furthermore, since the mull and tapes are completely hidden, there are no ridges ordinarily created by attaching them to the insides of the boards. Because split boards are usually thicker than single boards, their use is especially suited to thick, heavy books whose weight requires this added support and secure attachment. For maximum durability, split boards should be covered with cloth or buckram.

Four boards should be cut: a pair of lightweight ones, and another pair cut from heavier board. The thin boards go next to the signatures, with the tapes and mull attached to their outside surfaces. The heavier boards are then pasted to the thin ones, and the whole book put under *heavy* weights overnight for complete drying. After the boards have been cut to size, sand all the edges except those which will meet when the two layers are pasted together [FIG. 183].

Attach the thin boards as follows: lay the mull over onto a blank board (covered with wastepaper), and paste up the mull [FIG. 184]. Lay the tapes over onto the pasted mull, making sure they are at right angles to the back of the book. Paste the tapes [FIG. 185]. Pick up the pasted mull and tapes, and lay them over on top of the end sheet. Cover the work with a rubbing sheet, and rub it down [FIG. 186]. Trim off the fore-edge of this end sheet ¼ inch. Then put a clean sheet of wastepaper under the end sheet, and brush paste over the end sheet and the mull which is now fastened to it [FIG. 187]. Remove the soiled wastepaper. Now fold the end sheet back on itself, allowing the edge of it to come to within ¼ inch of the backbone [FIG. 188]. Cover the work with a rubbing sheet, and rub until dry. This flap, enclosing the tapes and mull, will go in between the two layers of board.

Lay this flap over on the blank board on a fresh piece of wastepaper, and paste up the inside of the flap [FIG. 189]. Next, lay the *thin* board in

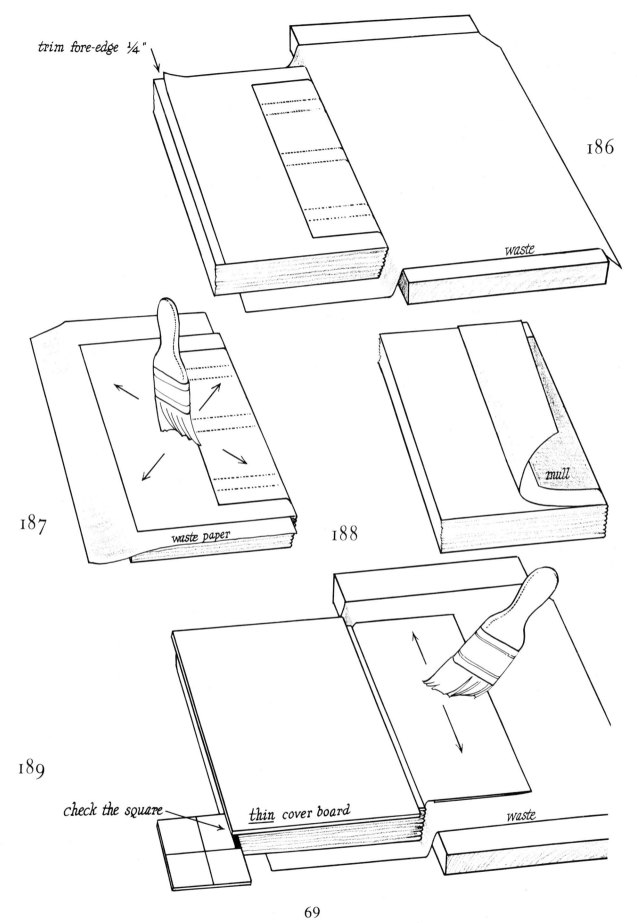

trim fore-edge ¼"

186

187

waste paper

188

mull

waste

189

check the square

thin cover board

waste

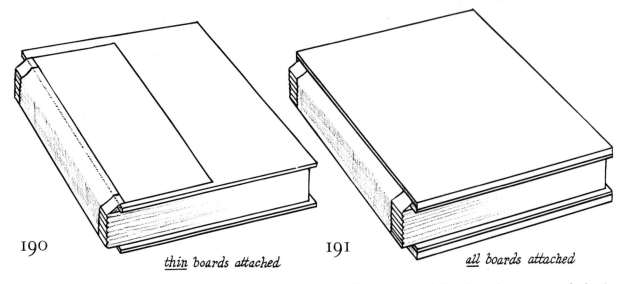

190   _thin_ boards attached   191   _all_ boards attached

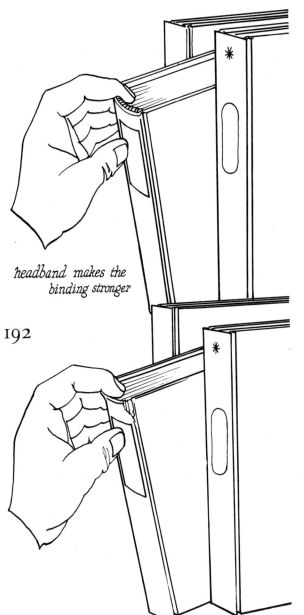

_headband makes the
binding stronger_

192

position on top of the first signature, and check the square on all three sides. Bring the pasted flap over on top of the board, and attach [FIG. 190]. Complete the split cover by pasting up the *thick* board and attaching it over the thin one. Be sure all the edges are in correct alignment. Put under weights for a half hour. Attach the other split boards in this same way [FIG. 191], then place the book under very heavy weights overnight. When the work is dry, lightly sandpaper the edges of the boards to remove any paste which has squeezed from the joints.

3. HEADBANDING

This is the process of reinforcing the head of the book by lacing a cord to the top of each signature by means of silk or cotton thread. Headbands were very common in old bindings which were sewn on three or more cords. Because a cord could not be sewn on too close to the head, the headband was devised as a means of "banding the head" tightly. In modern machine binding, a strip of woven headband material is simply glued across the backs of the signatures and serves only as decoration. But a true headband forms a strong cap, which protects the binding from the strain of pulling it from the bookshelf [FIG. 192]. It is especially recommended for a heavy book, such as a dictionary, as it distributes the pulling strain over all of the signatures, thus saving the cloth from tearing.

Headbanding is done after the signatures have been sewn onto tapes, and after the mull has been attached, but *before* attaching the boards. In the case of a round back binding, the headband is done after backing. A trial headband or two should be done on a discarded book as a preliminary preparation for a finished binding. Once an experimental headband has been completed, the procedure will be much more easily followed.

The headband is sewn on through a series of holes, punched beforehand in the center of

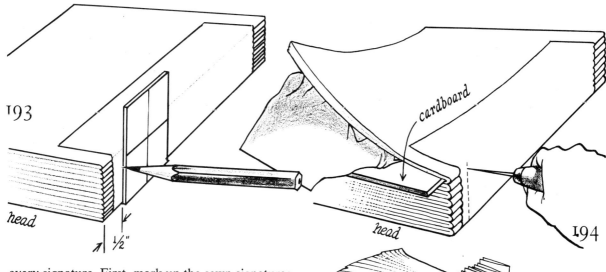

193

head

½"

194

cardboard

head

every signature. First, mark up the sewn signatures for punching. Stand the squared card against the back of the book, and draw a pencil line across all the signatures, about ½ or ⅝ inch down from the head [FIG. 193]. To punch the holes, lay a piece of cardboard inside the center of the first signature, and punch a hole with a small awl. Keep the awl level so the hole will come out in the center of the signature, against the edge of the cardboard [FIG. 194]. If the mull reaches close to the head, be careful to center the awl on the signature under it. Punch each of the signatures in this way. When the punching is completed, put a folded slip of paper in the center of each signature, for guide slips, then lock the book up in the press, standing it on end with the back facing one side [FIG. 195]. In this position, the head will be loose enough to permit convenient sewing.

Cut a piece of cord slightly smaller in diameter than the square of the book, and about four inches longer than the width of the backbone. Smooth cord is better than the sort with "whiskers" and a fairly soft cord is easier to manipulate than stiff twine. Wax the cord by drawing it across the cake of beeswax several times. Next thread a needle with a 12-inch length of *white* embroidery twist (silk is better than cotton). Thread a second needle with a similar length of *green* twist. Tie the ends of both threads together in a single knot. In making the headband of two different colors, the white will be sewn directly through each signature and around the cord, while the green will be used to wind the cord *between* signatures. The cord should be completely concealed by the alternate windings of the two colors.

Start the headband as follows: insert the folding needle inside the guide slip of the first signature. This merely locates the center of the signature and holds it open for easier working [FIG. 196]. Pick up the needle with the white thread (let the green hang free). Push the needle through the hole in the first signature, toward the

head

195

press

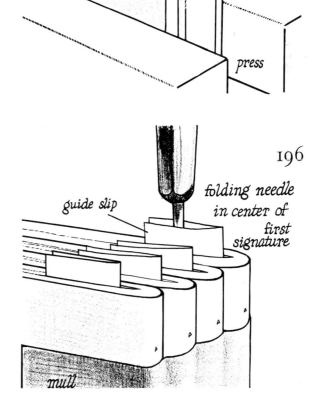

196

guide slip

folding needle in center of first signature

mull

center from the outside, at an angle toward the head of the book [FIG. 197]. Draw the white thread up until the knot is snug against the back of the signature [FIG. 198]. Lay the cord across the head of the book, and loop the white thread over it. Then pass the needle out through the *same hole,* as illustrated [FIG. 199]. Draw the white thread up

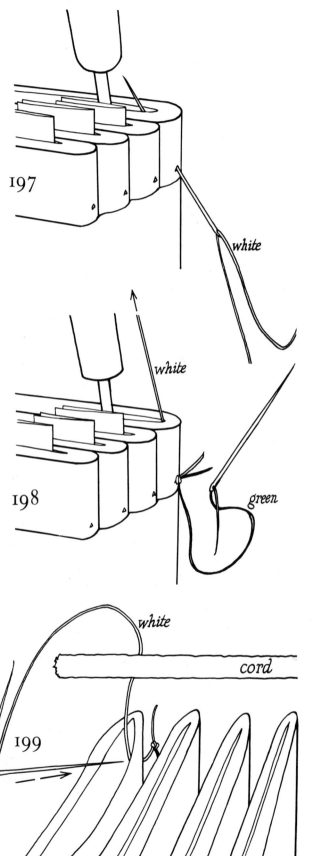

197

white

white

198

green

white

cord

199

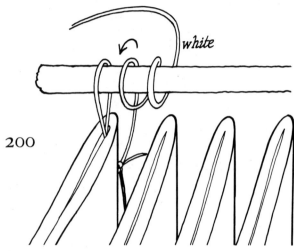

white

200

tight so that it holds the cord firmly down on top of the signature. At this point it is best to tie the white thread onto the starting knot, simply to keep this first stitch from working loose. Next, make two more loops of white around the cord [FIG. 200]. They should be touching each other and cover up the cord from view. To bind this much of the work together, the white thread is looped around *under* the cord [FIG. 201]; then the white

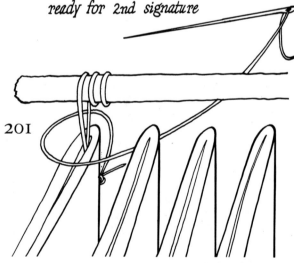

ready for 2nd signature

201

thread is carried down the back of the signature and tied onto the starting knot. This completes the first signature. The white thread attaches the cord to the signature, and the exact number of white loops depends on the thickness of the signature:

the combined white loops should equal this thickness. Now, the white thread is let fall free, and the *green* thread is used. The loops of green will fill the gap, or space, between the first signature and the second. These loops should also be set tightly one against the other. With the green thread, wrap two or more loops around the cord, working them

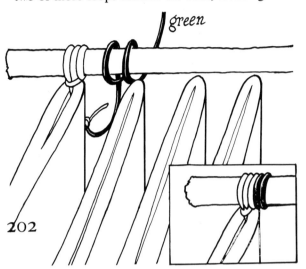

202

tightly against the white ones with the fingers [FIG. 202]. The number of green loops necessary to fill the gap will depend on the thickness of the signatures. If too few green loops are wrapped on, the signatures will be "pinched." After the green thread has been wrapped on, let it hang down free once more at the back of the signatures [FIG. 203].

Again pick up the white, and push the needle through the hole in the second signature, as before.

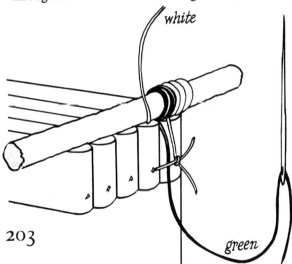

203

Let the white thread pass over the green which is hanging loose [FIG. 203]. Proceed to sew on the white thread as before. Then fill the next space with green. When the second signature is finished, the green thread is tied to the white where it

crosses from the first to the second signature, as illustrated [FIG. 204]. Each group of white stitches is finished by tying the white thread to the knot of the previous signature; every group of green stitches is finished by tying onto the crossing white strand. Proceed in this manner, working alternately with white and green, until the last signature

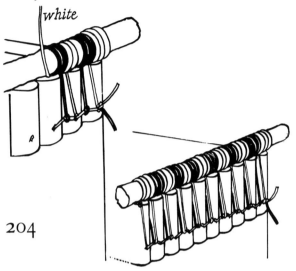

204

is finished. After the last knot has been tied, trim off both threads, leaving a ½-inch tail.

Leave the long ends of the cord until the boards have been attached. At that time, trim each end to within ⅛ inch of the silk winding. Touch the ends of the cord with paste to prevent raveling. The two ends of the headband cord should butt up against the edges of the boards in the finished binding [FIG. 205].

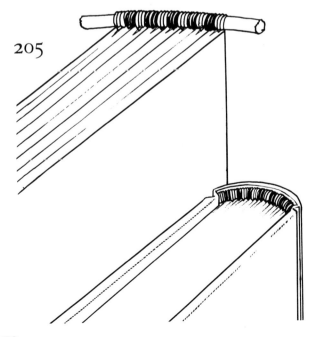

205

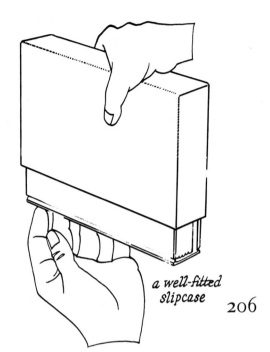

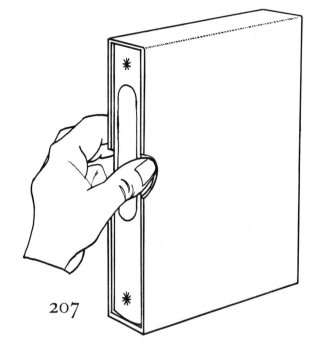

a well-fitted slipcase 206

207

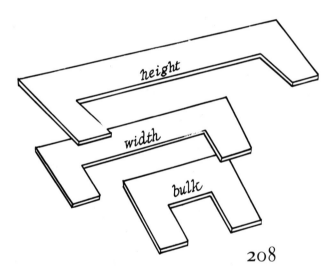

height

width

bulk

208

4. MAKING A SLIPCASE

A slipcase is a rigid box made to the book's exact dimensions and intended to protect it from damage of dust, excessive heat, and rough handling. New bindings will last much longer if a slipcase is made at the same time as the binding, and it holds the new work in proper place until all drying has taken place. Old and valuable volumes, such as first editions, should be fitted with slipcases to preserve them.

There are many styles of cases, but the one described here is simple, strong, and durable. Correct fitting is very important, or else the book will either be damaged or soiled in removing it from the case. Too loose a slipcase will cause the book to drop out and become damaged; too tight a case will require too much strain in pulling the book out. A properly fitted slipcase should permit the book to "slip" out when it is upended [FIG. 206]. The use of finger holes puts all the strain on the hinges of the book, and soils the binding as well [FIG. 207].

209

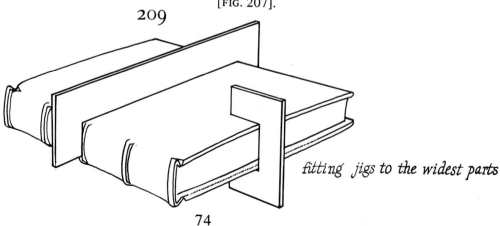

fitting jigs to the widest parts

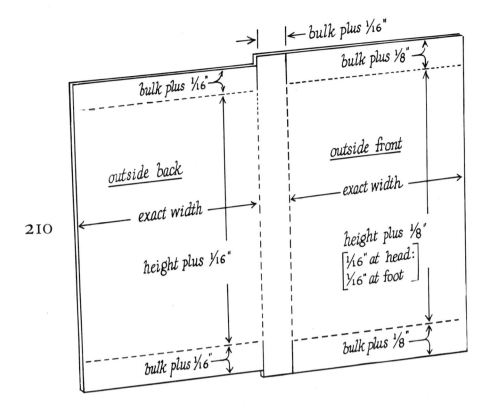

bulk plus 1/16"

bulk plus 1/8"

bulk plus 1/16"

210

outside back

outside front

← *exact width* →

← *exact width* →

height plus 1/16"

height plus 1/8"
[1/16" at head:
1/16" at foot]

bulk plus 1/16"

bulk plus 1/8"

ORDER OF WORK:
 Measure book to be cased
 Mark out cutting diagram
 Cut and score
 Line slipcase
 Fold up and paste
 Cover slipcase
 Press
 Make and attach label

The slipcase is made from a single sheet of lightweight board, such as illustration board. First measure the height, width, and the bulk of the book. From these measurements cut three jigs from cardboard [FIG. 208]. This is the most accurate means of assuring a proper fit. Fit each jig to the widest part of each dimension, trimming as necessary until the jig will slip easily over the book [FIG. 209]. If too much cardboard should be trimmed off, throw away the jig and make a new one.

Using the three finished jigs, lay out a cutting diagram on the sheet of illustration board, following the instructions in the illustration [FIG. 210].

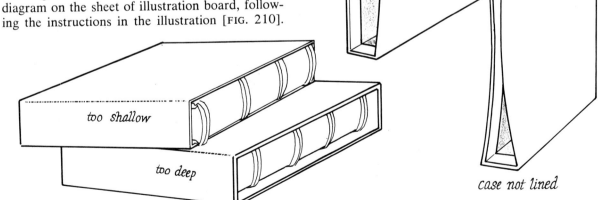

inaccurate measuring

case not lined

too shallow

too deep

75

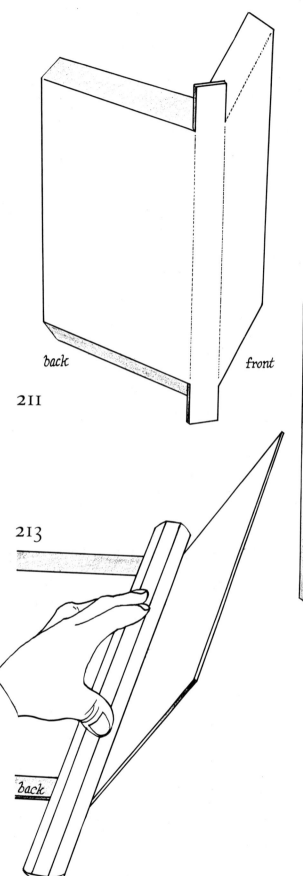

211

213

back   front

Since the case is actually one box folded inside another, an extra 1/16 inch is allowed at the head and at the foot of the front half of the case [FIG. 211]. The use of the steel square and a sharp 2H pencil is especially important here, or else the box will not be true. Using a sharp knife, cut out the slipcase; cut only on the solid lines of the illustration [FIG. 210]. The dotted lines indicate those edges which are to be scored and folded. However, do not fold up the case at this point. The inside of the slipcase is lined while it is still flat.

Select lining paper, and cut a single piece to fit the case, as in the illustration [FIG. 212]. Brush paste on the wrong side of the lining paper, and attach it to the case. Rub it down well, then put it under weights until dry.

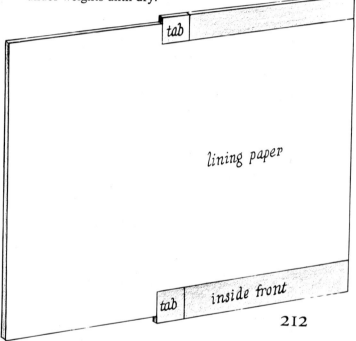

tab

lining paper

tab   inside front

212

When the attached lining is dry lay it flat on the bench, inside up. With the folding needle and ruler, score all lines which are shown as dotted lines [FIG. 210]. Now fold up the slipcase, using the ruler to guide the edges [FIG. 213].

To simplify pasting the case together, the work is done over a wooden last held in the finishing press (see Part 5, Making Tools and Equipment). Paste the four flaps of the case [FIG. 214], close up the case, and then place it over the last [FIG. 215]. The flaps of the back of the slipcase should fit *inside* those of the front [FIG. 216]. Using a clean cloth, rub the pasted flaps until they are dry. Keep the work tight against the last. Make certain that the edges of the flaps are even with the sides of the case. When the work is dry, wrap a length of gummed tape around the slipcase, draw it up tight and stick it to itself. Slide the

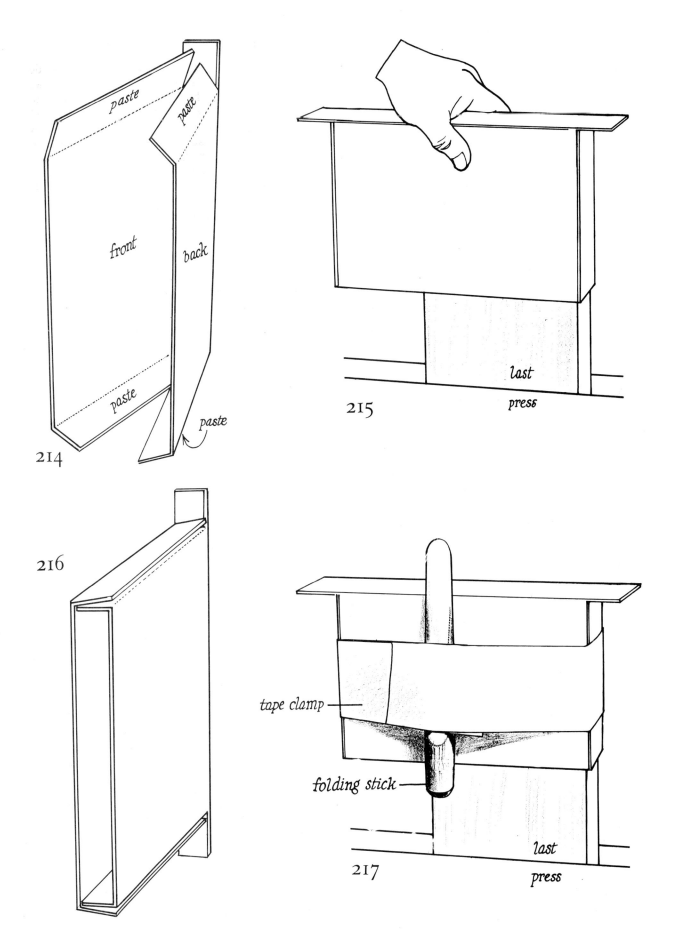

paste

paste

front

back

paste

paste

paste

214

215

last

press

216

tape clamp

folding stick

217

last

press

77

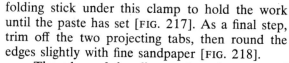

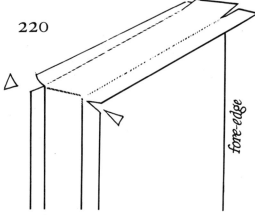

218

folding stick under this clamp to hold the work until the paste has set [FIG. 217]. As a final step, trim off the two projecting tabs, then round the edges slightly with fine sandpaper [FIG. 218].

The edges of the slipcase (top, bottom, and backbone) are covered with cloth. The sides are covered with paper—one panel for each side. Cut a piece of cloth the width of the backbone, plus one inch. Make it long enough to reach from the head fore-edge clear around to the foot fore-edge, with an extra ½ inch at each end. This will allow

220

fore-edge

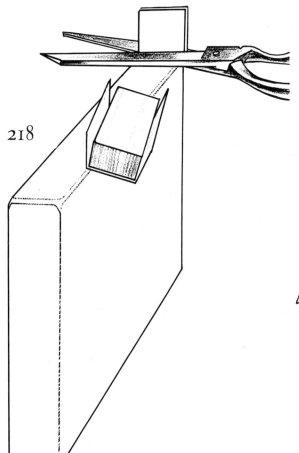

the cloth to turn over inside both fore-edges [FIG. 219]. Brush paste on the wrong side of the cloth, and let stand a minute; then paste again. Lay the pasted cloth on the top edge of the case—the ½-inch turnover projecting beyond the fore-edge. Smooth it down the backbone, and then attach it to the bottom edge. Check all sides to obtain a uniform overhang of ½ inch all around. Put the case over the last again, and rub the cloth well, using a clean cloth. With the shears, snip out the four corners of the cloth to provide a neat miter on

219

½"

½"

221

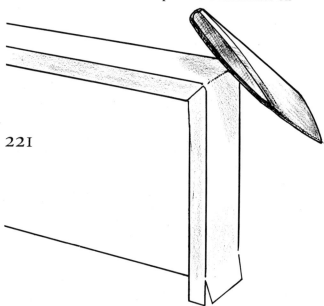

78

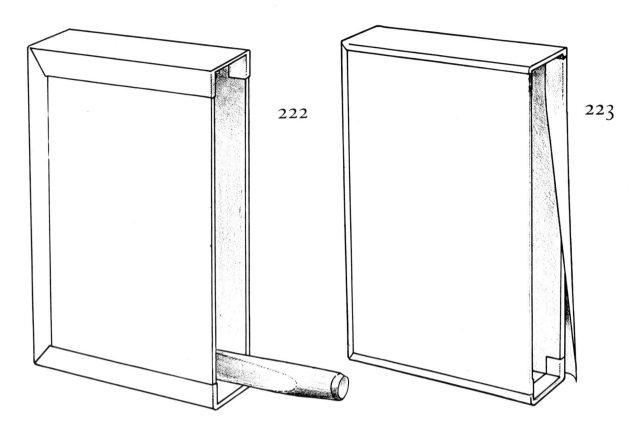

222

223

each corner. Slit the cloth at the fore-edges for turning in [FIG. 220].

Paste the turnover along the backbone, and attach both these flaps first. Then paste and turn over the remaining ones—the head and foot [FIG. 221]. Turn in the two flaps of cloth at the head and foot, creasing them well into the corners of the case with the edge of the folding stick [FIG. 222].

Cut two pieces of cover paper, one for each side panel. Allow a 1/8-inch margin on the three closed sides of the case, and add 1/2 inch to the fore-edge where it will turn inside the case [FIG. 223]. Paste and attach the side panels. Turn in the fore-edges and rub them gently until dry, using a clean cloth.

Wrap the book for which this case was made in waxed paper, and slip the book into the case. Protect the slipcase with waxed paper and put it under weights to dry [FIG. 224].

Make and attach the label (See Making Labels, p. 83).

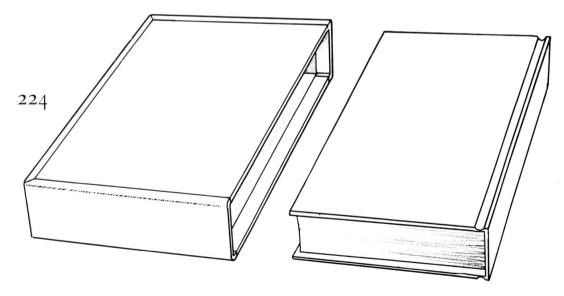

224

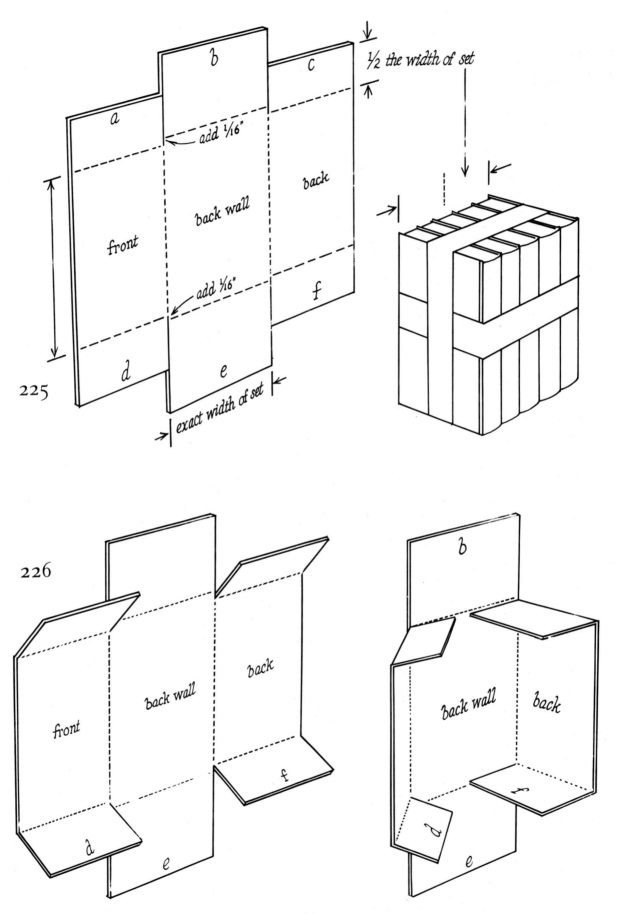

225

½ the width of set

b

c

a

add ⅟₁₆"

back

back wall

front

add ⅟₁₆"

f

d

e

exact width of set

226

back

front

back wall

f

d

e

b

Back wall

back

d

f

e

80

5. MAKING A BOX FOR A SET

ORDER OF WORK:

    Strap and measure set of books
    Mark out cutting diagram
    Cut and score
    Line inside of box
    Fold up and glue
    Cover outside of box
    Finish lining
    Make and attach label

The construction of a box to contain a set of books is essentially the same as that of a slipcase. The number of books in the set, as well as their size and weight, will govern the weight of board to be used. In the box described here the board is scored and folded to make a double layer at both the top and bottom. The lining is attached in two stages: the inside or back wall is lined while the box is still flat, and the remaining surfaces are lined after the box has been folded up and glued.

First, strap the set of books together with two lengths of gummed tape, preparatory to measuring. Measure the over-all height, width, and depth of the set. Then make three jigs (as described in the section on slipcases) to provide accurate dimensions.

Transfer the dimensions to a cutting diagram laid out on a single sheet of board. Use the steel square in making this diagram, following the plan in the illustration [FIG. 225]. The front and back sections of the box will be folded in, and the flaps of both these parts will be pasted to the top and bottom flaps [FIG. 226]. Cut out the box, according to the diagram, cutting only on the solid lines; the dotted lines represent edges to be folded up after the back wall has been lined. Then score all the lines which are dotted in the diagram.

Next, cut and attach the lining paper to the back wall of the box [FIG. 227]. Note that the

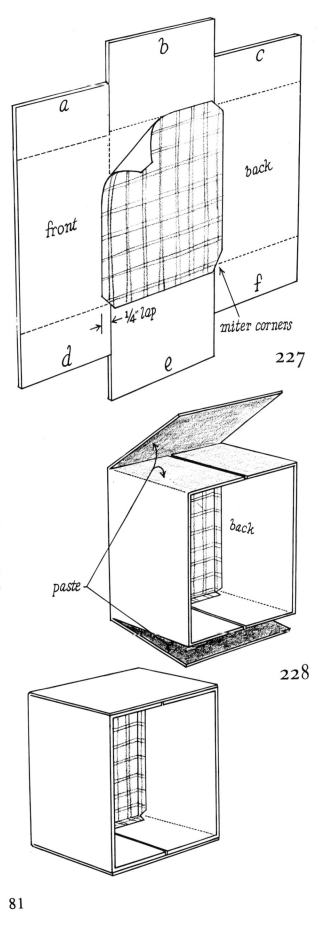

227

228

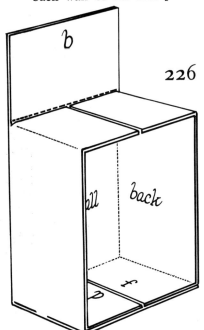

226

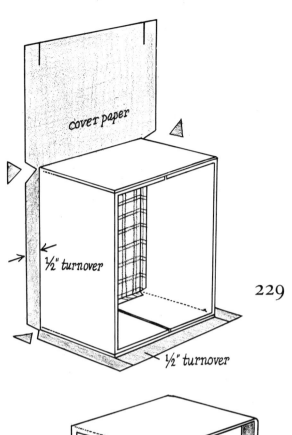

cover paper

½" turnover

½" turnover

229

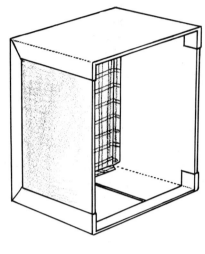

230

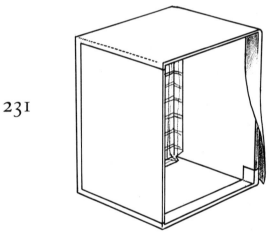

231

lining laps over all four folds ¼ inch, and that the four corners of this lining paper should be mitered. Then paste the flaps and join them, rubbing them down well [FIG. 228]. As the box cannot be conveniently placed on a last, it is easiest to stand the box upright on the bench and rub the joints dry from the inside of the box. The rubbing should be continued until the paste is dry. Finally, sand all the outside edges of the box lightly with fine sandpaper. This makes a smoother foundation over which the cover paper is attached.

Cut a single sheet of cover paper to cover the back, top, and bottom. The sides of the box are covered with two separate panels. Allow for a ½-inch turnover on the sides of the box, and at the fore-edges [FIG. 229]. Paste and attach the cover

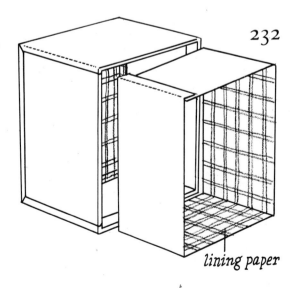

232

lining paper

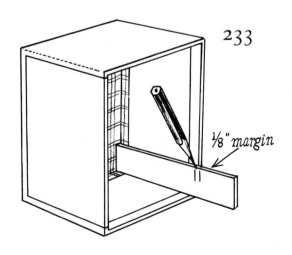

233

⅛" margin

paper, making sure the turnover is uniform on all sides. With the shears, snip out the four corners for mitering, and slit the fore-edge corners, as in the making of a slipcase. Paste and turn over these flaps. Turn the fore-edges over last, creasing the corners well with the folding stick [FIG. 230].

Cover the sides of the box with two separate panels of paper. Leave a ⅛-inch margin on the three closed sides of the box, and allow an extra ½ inch to turn in over the fore-edges [FIG. 231].

Now, line the rest of the inside of the box with a single strip of lining paper. Allow an extra ½ inch to lap under at the upper left corner [FIG. 232]. The lining should extend to within only ⅛ inch of the fore-edges of the box [FIG. 233]. Paste the lining and attach it, starting at the upper left corner. Smooth it down against the inside of the front of the box, and crease the paper well into the corners as you proceed. Keep the edge of the paper even with the back wall. With a clean cloth, rub all surfaces thoroughly to insure a secure attachment.

Finally, wrap the set of books in waxed paper to protect them from any paste spots, place them inside the box, and put the work under weights until dry.

Make and attach the label (see Making Labels, below).

6. MAKING LABELS

The label is a necessary part of bookbinding, since it is the means of identifying the work by title and author. Naturally, every book must have its title clearly attached. In the case of slipcases, boxed sets, folios, or music, the label may not be an essential requirement, although its use may add a desired decorative finish. For example, a set of boxed books, with each book clearly titled, would not need any further identification. The principal factor in deciding this is making the finished work useful and easily identified without unnecessary duplication. Whatever the particular labeling problem, the label should be simple, easy to read, and designed with the general character and appearance of the binding in mind.

ORDER OF WORK:
  Determine size and shape of label
  Make working sketch
  Mark out label
  Apply lettering
  Remove guide lines
  Varnish
  Cut out and attach
  Press

Professional looking labels may be made if the use of a small printing press, or hand press, is available. But even without this assistance,

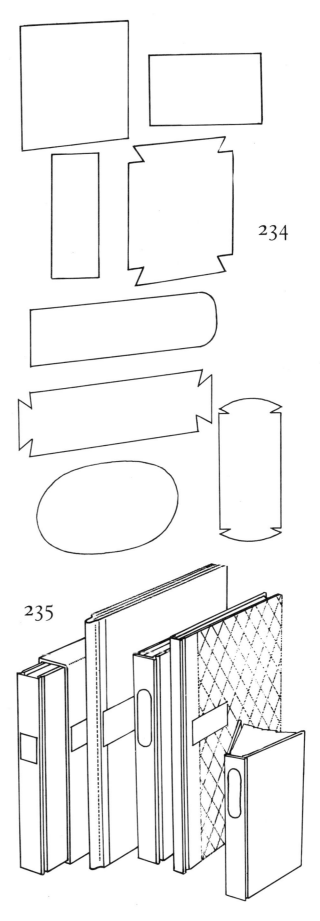

234

235

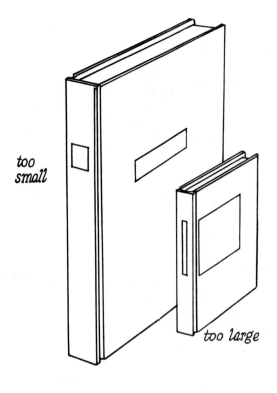

too small

too large

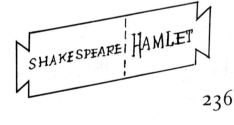

236

appropriate and attractive labels can be made with simple hand lettering. The wording of a label should include the full title of the book (with no abbreviations) and the author's name. If the original title included a sub-title, this may be omitted if space is small. Likewise, the author's last name may be used alone, if space does not permit the use of a long full name. In the case of music, the important information includes the composer's name, the title (and number) of the work, and possibly the name of the featured artist. Generally, the title of any work should be in the largest size letter, and the author's name smaller.

Simple, experimental labels should be tried out before making the finished one. These may be cut from ordinary typewriter paper, roughly sketched in, and then laid on the finished binding. Make several labels of different shapes and sizes to determine which one best fits the particular binding [FIG. 234].

A very slim volume of poetry may need only a simple rectangular label attached to the front board; in fact, it may be so slim that no other solution is possible. On a thicker book of some size, a backbone label with the title and author running horizontally may prove to be the best. A long title, especially, can often be most attractively accommodated by a narrow label with the lettering running up the length of the backbone [FIG. 235]. Bear in mind that hand-lettered labels require more space than printed ones and that it is more difficult to make small lettering than large.

With the size and shape worked out, make a trial working sketch, indicating the lettering roughly in pencil to decide on the proper size and emphasis [FIG. 236]. Then lay out the final work on good quality paper. Lightweight pen and ink paper will take pen lettering, and is equally good for brush work or colored ink. Avoid papers with a rough surface, or soft finish, as the paper fibers tend to clog the pen point. Thick, stiff paper is unsatisfactory because it is very difficult to paste it down securely.

Complete the lettering on a piece of paper larger than the final label. This makes it possible to use a triangle and the ruler to make the work square and true [FIG. 237]. With a 2H pencil, rule parallel guide lines, as well as a center line, to keep the lines of lettering of uniform size and properly spaced. The outline of an oval label can easily be laid out on the sheet of finished paper by first cutting a pattern, and then tracing inside it [FIG. 238]. Black waterproof india ink is the most permanent lettering fluid. If, however, you wish to use a second color in conjunction with black, you may use opaque watercolor or tempera [FIG. 239].

The lettering should be done with clean

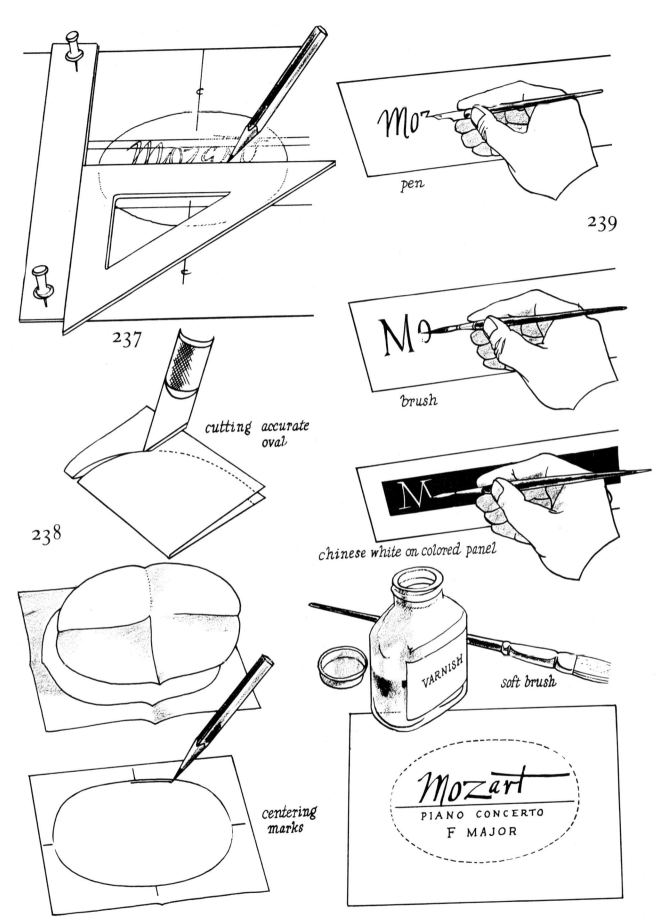

237

238

cutting accurate oval

239

pen

brush

chinese white on colored panel

centering marks

soft brush

VARNISH

Mozart
PIANO CONCERTO
F MAJOR

240

strokes. If you make an error, discard the label and start a fresh one. Any clean-up work done with Chinese white will show up very clearly!

When the lettering is completed, put it aside until thoroughly dry. Then clean off all the pencil guide lines with an Artgum eraser, but leave those which outline the shape of the label! Then, brush a very thin coat of retouching varnish over the lettering, covering the entire label area out past the edges. Allow the varnish to dry overnight. The label may be cut out with the shears or a sharp knife [FIG. 240].

Attach the label to the binding, using map-mounting paste or binder's paste. Brush paste on the back of the label, making sure the edges are given a final brushing. Lay the label in position on the binding. When attaching a backbone label, put the book, back up, in the finishing press. Keep the label from slipping, once it has been laid on the binding. Any smear of paste will be almost impossible to remove without leaving a stain on the binding. Cover the label with a clean rubbing sheet and very gently rub until dry. Place the work under weights overnight to dry. If the label is a backbone label, a clamp may be put over the work to hold it tightly during drying. Use a strip of gummed tape, drawn securely over the backbone, and under the jaws of the press [FIG. 241].

The same principles apply to labels made on a printing press. The size of type should be chosen with the character of the book in mind, as well as the size of the book. The letter spacing should be worked out on a rough pencil sketch before the type is set. Careful make-ready is very important, so that the impression will be uniformly black on every letter. When printing the final work, make a dozen proofs, then select the one which is the most uniformly black and crisp. *Allow the ink to dry overnight* before cutting out the label and attaching it.

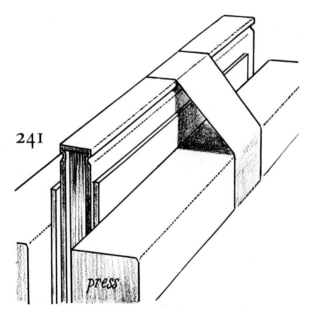

241

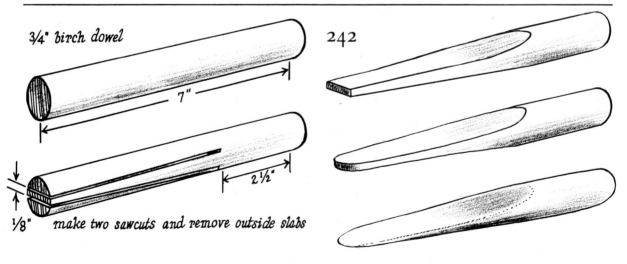

242

3/4" birch dowel

7"

2½"

1/8"   make two sawcuts and remove outside slabs

PART 5
Making Tools and Equipment

ALL OF THE TOOLS AND EQUIPMENT ESSENtial to good hand binding may be obtained from one of the bookbinding supply houses. Their equipment is of professional quality, manufactured from the best materials, and designed especially for the small hand binding shop, schools, or the individual who does a considerable amount of binding. Because of its high quality, this equipment is somewhat expensive, especially the sewing frame and finishing press, the two most critical items on the list. However, commercially manufactured equipment will last indefinitely. And the initial cost may be reduced if group purchasing is considered.

This chapter is included for those who have the skill, as well as the interest, for making their own tools. All of the equipment described here is serviceable for the binding procedures outlined in the book. The various tools can be made from currently available woods and metals, and if carefully made will perform work of professional quality. Historically considered, the bookbinder's tools and his methods have not changed very much since early binders made their own by hand. Many people still share their satisfaction in making the tools of the trade.

The accompanying diagrams are sufficiently self-explanatory for making the different tools, although a few general recommendations should

be observed. Use only the best grade of kiln-dried hardwoods, such as maple, birch, beech, or walnut. Sharpen all woodworking tools to razor keenness, and hone their cutting edges when necessary during the work. Use a steel carpenter's square, the try square, or a miter box to obtain square and accurate cuts. Cut all edges a little full, then finish them to dimension with a sharp plane and fine sandpaper. The sharp edges of wood should be slightly rounded with fine sandpaper.

Warped or twisted equipment will not produce good results; therefore, wood should be selected carefully, and as soon as it has been cut and sanded, a coat of sealer should be applied to seal out moisture. This finish may then be rubbed down with fine steel wool to obtain a smooth finish.

In joining wooden parts, use a combination of screws and a good *waterproof* glue, holding the work in iron clamps until the glue is dry. Any metal parts, such as bolts and nuts, should be cleaned with naptha to remove the coating of machine grease; and the nuts should be run back and forth on their bolts a few times to make sure there are no burrs to obstruct the free operation of the finished equipment.

All the binding tools and equipment are used in connection with very fragile materials—paper, cloth, thread, and cardboard. For this reason it is

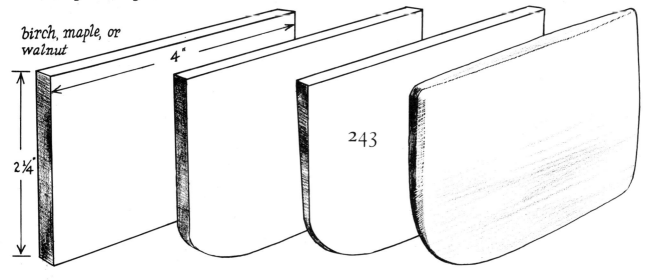

birch, maple, or walnut

4"

2¼"

243

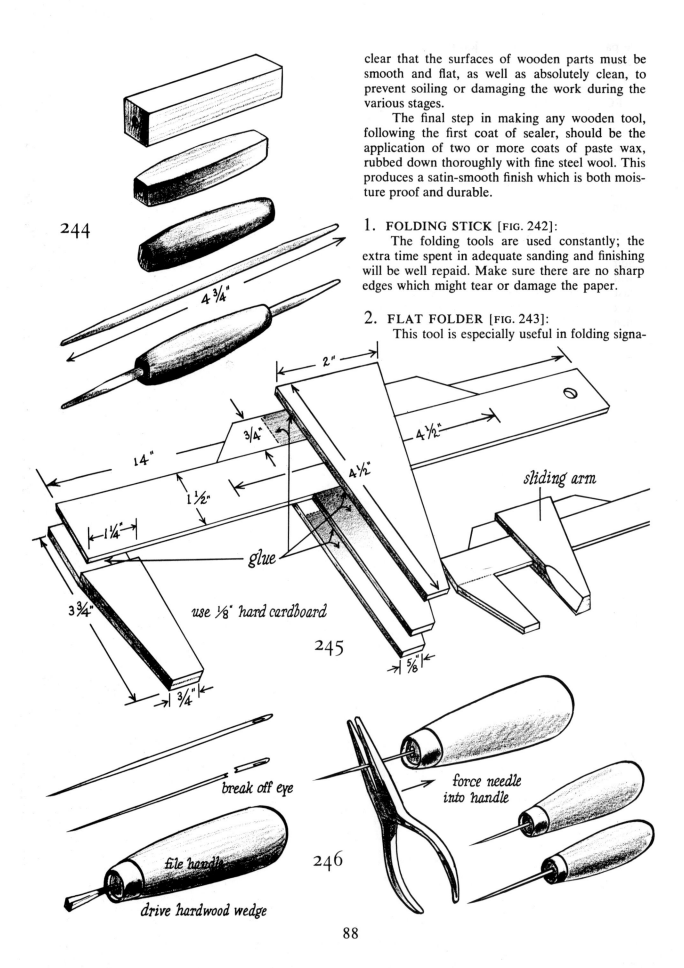

clear that the surfaces of wooden parts must be smooth and flat, as well as absolutely clean, to prevent soiling or damaging the work during the various stages.

The final step in making any wooden tool, following the first coat of sealer, should be the application of two or more coats of paste wax, rubbed down thoroughly with fine steel wool. This produces a satin-smooth finish which is both moisture proof and durable.

1. FOLDING STICK [FIG. 242]:

The folding tools are used constantly; the extra time spent in adequate sanding and finishing will be well repaid. Make sure there are no sharp edges which might tear or damage the paper.

2. FLAT FOLDER [FIG. 243]:

This tool is especially useful in folding signa-

244

4¾"

2"

4½"

14"

3/4"

4½"

sliding arm

1½"

1¼"

glue

use ⅛" hard cardboard

3¾"

245

5/8"

3/4"

break off eye

force needle into handle

file handle

246

drive hardwood wedge

88

ture paper and does a better job than the folding stick. In working the sides down to the flat bevel, keep the surfaces free of ridges.

3. FOLDING NEEDLE [FIG. 244]:

This is an indispensable tool for fine work in tight places on such work as mitering corners and turning in paper on slipcases. It performs the function of an extra finger of the hand. A steel knitting needle has a smooth surface and at the same time is strong enough to perform as an ideal scoring tool.

4. BOOK CALIPERS [FIG. 245]:

This is not essential unless a great amount of binding is contemplated. But, made with accuracy, it will save a great deal of time in taking precise measurements in all of the principal binding steps. The critical part of this tool is the sliding arm, which must move freely but without any wobble.

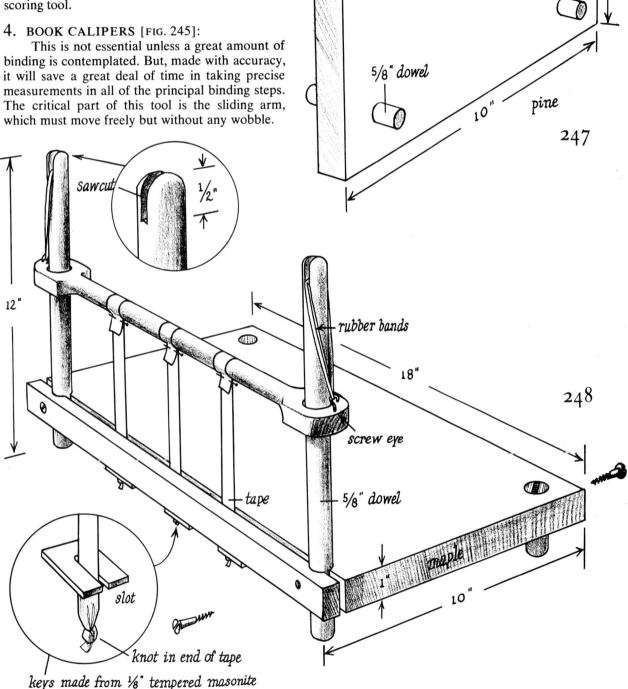

8"

5/8" dowel

10" pine

247

12"

sawcut   ½"

rubber bands

18"

248

screw eye

tape   5/8" dowel

slot

maple

1"

10"

knot in end of tape

keys made from ⅛" tempered masonite

89

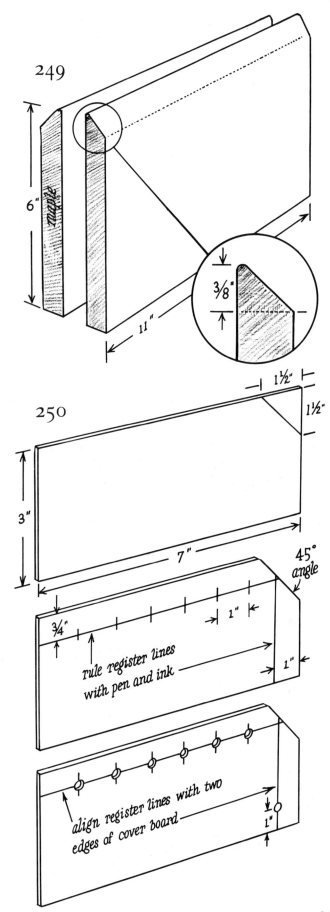

5. AWLS [FIG. 246]:

Handmade awls of the type illustrated are superior to the commercial ones, most of which have too large a shaft. Because the hole which an awl makes should be slightly smaller than the thread used, it is preferable to make two or three awls from steel sewing needles, fitted into file handles or wooden ones of your own construction. In this way you can easily obtain a very fine awl exactly suited to the work at hand.

6. PUNCH BOARD [FIG. 247]:

Simple though it is, this piece of equipment, when used in conjunction with the finishing press, helps perform certain binding steps more easily and more accurately.

7. SEWING FRAME [FIG. 248]:

A frame of this size will accommodate all but the largest books, and properly constructed is equal in performance to a ready-made one. The sewing tapes are held in place under the slot in the platform by keys, which may be made from metal or thin hardwood such as maple. The wooden screw posts used in commercial frames are more convenient than the elastic used in the frame illustrated; but this substitute has proven quite satisfactory.

8. BACKING BOARDS [FIG. 249]:

These are used when backing a book, after it has been rounded. In this operation, performed with the backing hammer, these boards are subjected to heavy strain, and should therefore be made from hard maple. The pair illustrated are designed to fit the finishing press described below; the important thing is to make them slightly shorter than the distance between the two screws of the finishing press. Round the top edges carefully so that the shoulders formed along the signatures of the book will be bent, and not cut.

9. MITERING JIG [FIG. 250]:

Select a hard, dense cardboard about 3/16 inch thick, or, if you have metal working tools, a flat sheet of brass. This tool must be made to very exacting standards or its time saving function will be lost. Mark out a cutting diagram, using the steel square, and cut it out with great care. Locate and rule the two register lines with pen and india ink. Then after positioning the seven holes, punch out the holes with a paper punch. Check the finished jig with a try square: if there are any flaws, discard it and make another one.

10. WOODEN LASTS [FIG. 251]:

These are so simple to make that it will be worth the time involved, even if you expect to make only a few slipcases. Made of pine, two or three sizes should be made to accommodate slipcases of various dimensions. When making a slip-

90

case over a last, use the size which is slightly thinner than the width of the case.

11. BLANK BOARDS [FIG. 252]:

Three or four blank boards are almost essential to support a binding while the work is in progress. For example, when pasting down the end sheets or attaching lining papers, the blank board holds the cover of the book firmly and prevents any strain on the unfinished hinges. The three sizes illustrated will handle almost any situation, either individually or in combination.

12. SQUARED CARD [FIG. 253]:

The card illustrated is three inches square and cut from a piece of good quality illustration board, which is white on both sides. On a sheet of board lay out a cutting diagram, using the steel square to make all four corners exactly *square*. Before cutting out the card, rule two crossing lines on the card with pen and ink to divide it into four equal squares. Then rule a black band along *one* outside edge of each of the squares, each band of a different width. Mark each square with its designated width, following the illustration. The reverse side of the card should be prepared in the same way; make sure that bands of similar width are back-to-back.

13. RIGHT ANGLE CARD [FIG. 254]:

This cardboard tool is primarily useful for squaring the head, just before gluing up. A try square will perform the same function, although this card is less clumsy to use. The vital part of its manufacture is the inside angle, which must be perfectly square.

14. FINISHING PRESS [FIG. 255]:

This press will perform very satisfactory work. It should be substantial and quite heavy. The weight of the press will prevent its moving about on the bench during some of the heavier tasks such as backing.

The two holes (in both jaws of the press) which house the long bolts must be accurately bored. If they cannot be bored on a drill press, first make a jig by boring a ⅝-inch hole in a piece of two-inch stock. Then clamp this block to the face of the jaw, and in correct position, to guide the bit.

Crank arms made from ¼-inch rod may be welded to the heads of the two bolts for more rapid operation of the press. Whereas a commercially made press is constructed so the screws open, as well as close the jaws, this press requires the jaws to be pulled open by hand. But because this is one of the most expensive pieces of equipment, this drawback does not prove too much of a disadvantage.

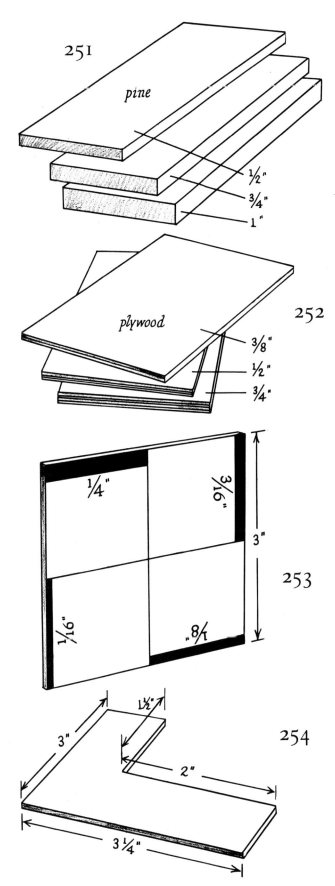

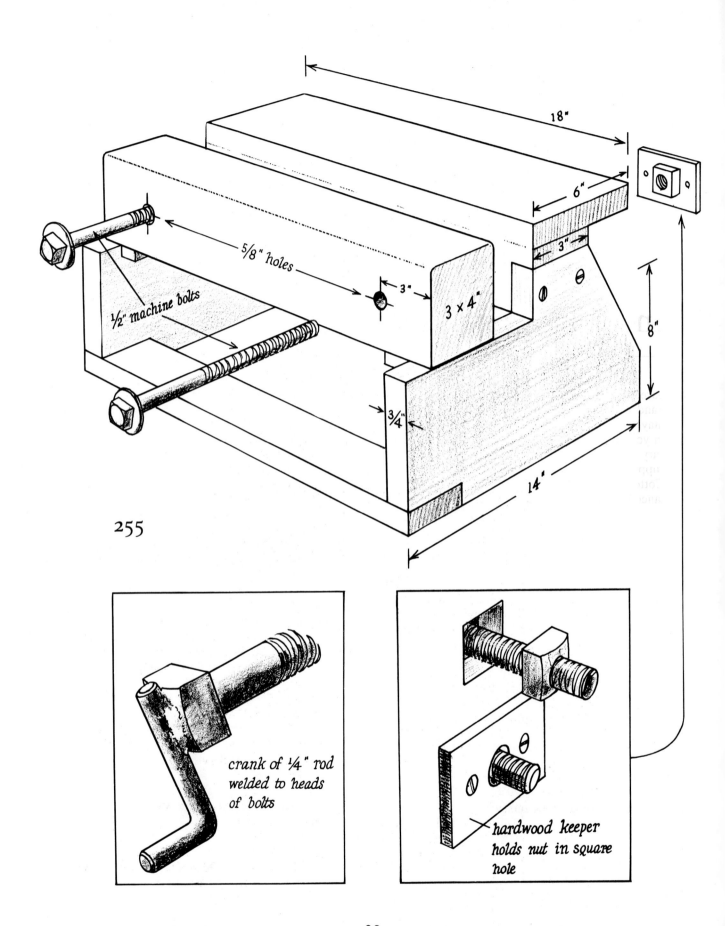

18"

6"

3"

5/8" holes

3"

3 × 4"

8"

1/2" machine bolts

3/4"

255

14"

crank of 1/4" rod welded to heads of bolts

hardwood keeper holds nut in square hole

Index to Suppliers

Most of the suppliers listed below are prepared to furnish materials in small quantities to hand bookbinders. The names of other suppliers may be found in the classified telephone directory in your local area. In addition, some of the necessary tools and materials can be obtained from art supply dealers, and in hardware and craft stores. Cotton and linen tape and cloth, pins, and miscellaneous items are available in department stores.

Andrews-Nelson-Whitehead Boise Cascade
Paper Distribution
7 Laight Street
New York, N.Y.
 Domestic and imported decorative papers, oriental and art papers, cover papers, lining papers from European and Scandinavian countries. Samples available.

Carter, Rice, Storrs & Bement, Inc.
273 Summer Street
Boston, Massachusetts
 Strathmore and other fine printing and specialty papers, and cover papers.

Craftools, Inc.
1 Industrial Avenue
Woodbridge, New Jersey
 Complete line of domestic and imported tools, equipment, and materials for hand bookbinding: everything necessary, including needles, thread, papers, boards, and adhesives.

A. I. Friedman
25 West 45th Street
New York, N.Y.
 Brushes, knives, pastes, varnish, vegetable glue, pencils, pens. A wide selection of boards, illustration boards, colored cover papers, and other specialty papers.

J. L. Hammet Company
48 Canal Street
Boston, Massachusetts
 Sphinx paste, binders board, kraft paper, folders, needles, thread, and other items.

W. O. Hickok Mfg. Company
9th & Cumberland Streets
Harrisburg, Pennsylvania
 Professional equipment for large scale hand binding: sewing frames, presses, plows, and hand tools. Catalog.

Morningstar-Paisley, Inc.
630 West 51st Street
New York, N.Y.
 Map mounting glue for guarding, mending, repairing, and attaching labels.

Technical Library Service
104 Fifth Avenue
New York, N.Y.
 General supplies and information.

Transparo Company
P.O. Box 838
New Rochelle, N.Y.
 Transparent, 100% silk mending material for guarding and repairing.

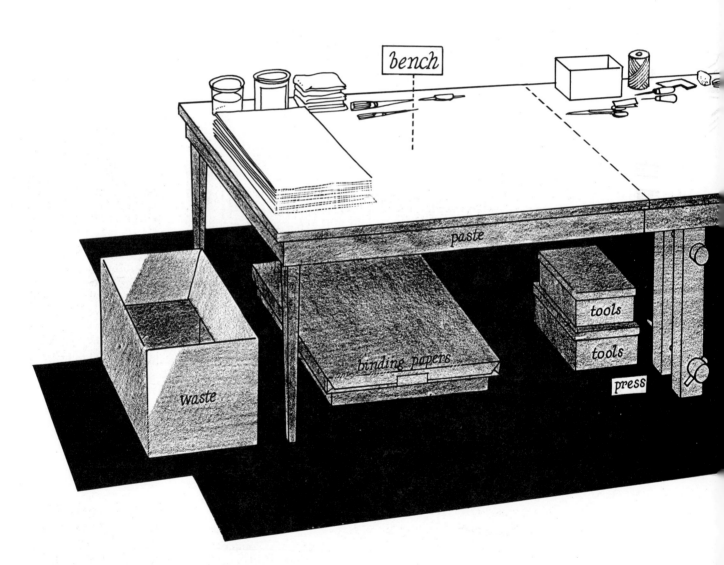

bench

paste

tools

tools

binding papers

waste

press

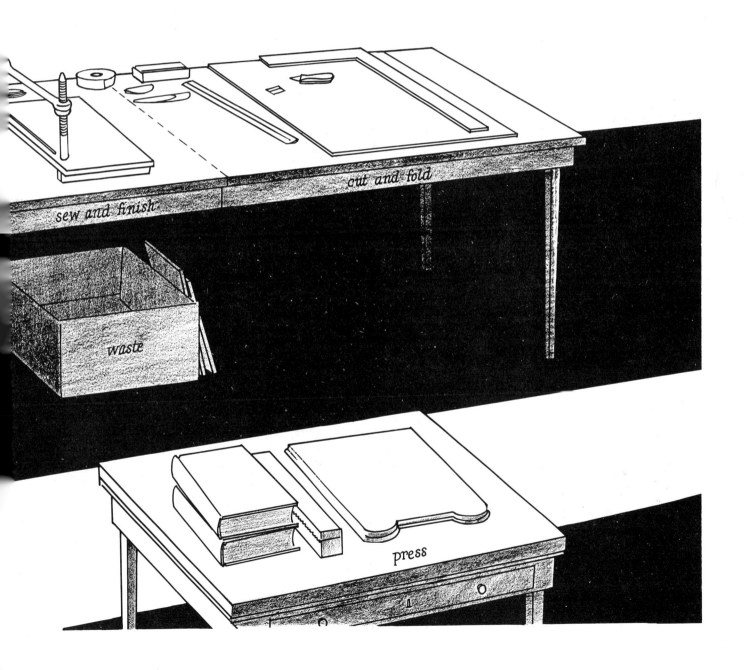

sew and finish

cut and fold

waste

press